EDEXCEL GCSE POETRY ANTHOLOGY

ANTHOLOGY

COLLECTION C: Time & Place

Cover: Westminster, January, 1st, 2017

Contents

About the Author

After graduating from Oxford University with a degree in English Language and Literature, and 26 years working for British Airways, I decided to train as a teacher of English. For the next ten years, I taught in the secondary state sector in a multi-cultural and socio-economically diverse area west of London. On my retirement in 2016, I was second in the English department, co-ordinator of the A Level English Literature curriculum and Lead Year 13 tutor, co-ordinating university entrance applications. I am also an Examiner for AQA GCSE English Literature.

My approach to studying poetry is straightforward: unless you understand *what is happening* in the poem – the event, incident or story – about which the poet weaves his literary magic, there can be no understanding of a poet's literary techniques. The two are inextricably intertwined. There is a LOT of very variable analysis of poetry on the internet. Much of it stems from a failure to understand *what is happening*. This failure leads to students having a rattle-bag of literary terminology with nothing on which to hang it. Naming metric forms and rhyme schemes, and poetic techniques, with no understanding of why the poet has used them, is a waste of time. It also leads to spurious, and erroneous, analyses of structure and form. I have read, in exam papers, that the *"shape of the line on the page, if you turn it sideways, corresponds to the furrows of a field."* Or, *"the varied line length suggests the outline of the Manhattan skyline"*. Students do not come up with ideas like this unless there is a fundamental failure to grasp the links between *substance (*the *"what is happening")* and *structure (*rhythm and rhyme*)* and *language (*the words used*)*.

This guide is an attempt to make these links and help students appreciate why a poem has been written in the way that it has.

About this Guide

The Guide has been written primarily for students of GCSE English Literature as specified by EDEXCEL in the post-2015 syllabus (1ET0). It addresses the requirement to study one cluster of poems taken from the *EDEXCEL/Pearson Poetry Anthology* and the requirement to analyse and compare two Unseen poems. These requirements are assessed in Component 2 (19th century Novel and Poetry since 1789), Section B: Poetry, and Section C: Unseen Poetry, of the examination.

The Guide aims to address Assessment Objectives AO1, AO2 and AO3 for the examination of this component, namely:

AO1: Read, understand and respond to texts. Students should be able to:
- maintain a critical style and develop an informed personal response
- use textual references, including quotations, to support and illustrate interpretations. [*1]

---

[1] *Whilst there is no specific mention of *"making comparisons"*, the mark scheme makes it clear that the examiners expect the essay response to be *"comparative"*, described as *"Critical, exploratory comparison"* at the highest band.

AO2: Analyse the language, form and structure used by a writer to create meanings and effects, using relevant subject terminology where appropriate.

AO3: Show understanding of the relationships between texts and the contexts in which they were written.

The poems are explored individually, with links and connections between them drawn as appropriate. The format of each exploration is similar:

- An explanation of key features of the poem that require contextual knowledge or illustration and the relationship between the text and its context.
- A summary of the key themes of the poems, with a note on possible thematic links to other poems in the cluster
- A summary of the metric form, rhyme scheme or other structural features, related to the theme
- A "walk-through" (or explication) of the poem, ensuring that what is happening in the poem is understood, how the rhythm and rhyme contribute to meaning, an explanation of the meaning of words which may be unfamiliar, an exploration of language and imagery and a comment on main themes.

A note on "themes" (AO1 task)

The question (or *task*) in the examination for *Component 2 (19th century Novel and Poetry since 1789), Section B: Poetry,* will be on a *theme or topic* which may form the focus of the poem or be an integral part of its meaning. You will be asked to make a comparative exploration of the presentation of this *"theme"* or topic in one named poem and one other poem of your choice from the collection.

Section C: Unseen Poetry will ask you to explore the presentation of a given *"theme"* or topic in an Unseen poem and compare it to the treatment of the same *theme* in a second Unseen poem.

Less commonly, the question in either Section may ask you to write on the use of a particular *poetic technique,* such as *imagery*.[2]

Given that Collection C is titled *"Time & Place"*, you can expect to be asked to explore various ideas and perspectives on this theme. This could include, but not be limited to: **memories of significant places or times** in the poets' lives; the **evocation**[3] of **"place"**, as the subject of the poem, or as the setting for the poem; the

---

[2] The use of *metaphor, simile, personification* etc. or language appealing to the five senses.
[33] *Evocation* (noun) and *evokes* (verb) are useful words in describing poetry. It means, literally, *"calling out"* or describing vividly.

treatment (including use of poetic techniques) of **abstract concepts** such as Memory, Alienation, Displacement or Home; a "**happening**" such as Emigration, Death, Separation, a Journey. The range is very broad.

Where a poem from the collection lends itself to suggesting a particular theme or topic, this has been noted in the overview and linked to other poems which have similar themes. However, these suggestions are illustrative, not exhaustive; one of the skills to be mastered is to know the texts well enough to be able to link them to themes which may not be immediately obvious. Students should spend some time mapping the links between poems thematically and illustrating how these themes are treated in similar or differing ways.

As well as links of *theme,* links and connections should be made between *narrative voice, form, structure* and *language.* At the end of this book are some questions which should be considered when making links and connections, and when analysing the Unseen (see "*Links and Connections.*")

A note on "relevant subject terminology" (AO1)

This means the *semantic field* of literary criticism, or "jargon". There is a language to describe the features of literature, just as football has words to describe manoeuvres and equipment – "*penalty*", "*off-side*", "*wing*", "*long cross*", "*throw-in*". To be able to critique literature, you need to know this language and use it correctly. Throughout this guide, literary terminology has been *italicised*, indicating that these words need to become part of your vocabulary when discussing the texts and writing essays. For illustration, here are some very basic literary terms that are often carelessly used and will make your writing in exams less effective if you do not apply them correctly.

Text – is the printed words. The *whole text* is all the words that are identified, usually by a *title*, as belonging together as an integral piece of writing.

A *book* is a collection of printed pages bound together to make a *whole text*. A *book* can be any text – fiction, non-fiction; play, novel; car maintenance manual, encyclopaedia. A *book* is a **physical** entity, like "*DVD*" or "*scroll*", not a creative one.

A *novel* is a type of text – a *genre*. It is characterised by certain creative features, such as being *fictional,* usually *narrative in structure* and with various *characters* who do things, or have things happen to them. It may be *descriptive* and may contain *dialogue*.

A *novella* is a short novel. The scope and the number of characters are often (but not always) more limited than in a novel.

A *short story* is a narrative fiction, of variable, but limited length.

A *play* is another *genre*. It is designed to be performed and watched, rather than read. It can be *fictional* or *non-fictional*, or a mixture. It is predominantly made up of *dialogue* between *characters*, although there may be descriptive elements within this *dialogue* and in the *stage directions*.

A *poem* is a particular *genre* which is characterised by the deliberate, and recurring, use of *rhythm* and *rhyme* and/or by a particular attention to *diction*, in the form of *word-choice* and *imagery*. It is opposed to *prose*. However, there are *poetical* prose writers whose language uses the distinctive features of poetry – such as *alliteration*, *rhythm* and *imagery*.

Beyond these simple definitions, there are a host of other literary terms. These terms have been used where they are necessary to describe features of the texts and are defined on the first usage, and subsequently when repeated, depending on how common the usage and the relevance to the poem under discussion.

There is a trend towards teaching students grammatical terms – such as the parts of speech – and using these in essays, in the mistaken belief that these will gain marks under use of "*subject terminology*". This achieves very little. The feedback from the Examining Boards make it clear that linguistic analyses, including analyses of parts of speech, have little merit when demonstrating *critical understanding*. It is also better to avoid using subject terminology if you are unsure of its exact meaning.

A note on "critical comparisons" (AO1)

The new specification refers to "*links and connections*" as well as "*comparisons*" between literary texts. There is little to be gained from making spurious comparisons which fail to illuminate the text, and structuring essays which say, *"on the one hand/ on the other"*. The highest band marks challenge the student to be able to *synthesise* their knowledge of the texts – a higher level skill. The Mark Scheme refers to: *"critical, exploratory, well-structured comparison"*. Further guidance on this is given in the section on *"Links and Connections"*.

A note on "create meanings and effects" (AO2)

There are very few marks to be gained by simply spotting and correctly naming literary techniques. Even fewer if those terms are used incorrectly. It is better NOT to use a literary term at all than use the wrong one. **NEVER build an essay around literary techniques; you need to focus your essay on the thematic question (the *"task"*), showing how form, structure and language contribute to meaning**. Comments on literary techniques **must** be linked to purpose and meaning to gain marks in the higher bands. This principle has been followed in the analyses of the texts. Only those literary techniques that are particularly relevant to the discussion of meaning, form or theme have been explored.

You are also required to know something about *metric form* – the use of rhythm and the terms which are used to describe it – and relate the use of *metre* to meaning. Metre has been explained in the commentaries. Stressed beats are in **bold** and the *metric feet* are shown with the / symbol. *"A Note on Metre"* has been given at the end of this guide, which explains the main metric forms used, with examples from the texts.

Finally, you need to know when form and structure are used *for effect* and when the choice of a form or structure is part of a poetic tradition or a feature of a poetic movement (e.g. *Romantic, Modern*). Sometimes poets write in *sonnet* form because they like writing *sonnets*; they are following a tradition; it was expected by their readers at the time of writing. Similarly, with choices of metre. Both *iambic pentametre* and *ballad form* (alternating lines of *iambic tetrametre* and *iambic trimetre*) are common metric forms[4] used by very many poets of different eras because it was a common form for poetry. It *may* be valid to link the choice of metric form to the poet's theme and it *may* be that the poet uses the metric form within the poem for effect. However, making far-fetched and spurious connections between choice of form and theme are largely a waste of time. Sometimes a *sonnet* is just a *sonnet*. However, *how* (rather than *why*) the *sonnet* form is used in a poem should be explored. For example, where the *volta*[5] occurs, the use of rhyme and the use of rhyming *couplets*, and these choices related to meaning.

A note on "relationship between texts and context" (AO3)

There is a requirement to have some knowledge of the biographical, socio-economic, political or literary

---

[4] Explanations of these terms are given throughout the text and in the section *"A Note on Metre"* at the end.
[5] The *volta* is the "turn" or switch in the argument of the poem

context in which these poems were written **and show how this is reflected in the text.** "Context" is also taken to mean *"ideas and perspectives".* This may include understanding the relationship between the specific themes of the poem and the more general attitudes of society at the time. Edexcel has given further guidance:

- *the author's own life and individual situation, including the place and time of writing, only where these relate to the text*
- *the historical setting, time and location of the text*
- *social and cultural contexts (e.g., attitudes in society; expectations of different cultural groups)*
- *the literary context of the text, for example, literary movements or genres*
- *the way in which texts are received and engaged with by different audiences, at different times (for example, how a text may be read differently in the twenty-first century from when it was written).*

Understanding of meaning is enriched by knowing relevant autobiographical details, particularly where the subject matter focuses on relationships. Many poems use allusions and references to classical mythology, the Bible, popular culture and general knowledge, without which meaning is obscure and appreciation limited.

Relevant contextual information has been given for each poem in either the introduction under "**Context**" or in the analyses.

A note on *typography*

Typography is the way the words of the poems are printed on the page. Remember – most poems, until relatively recently, were written by hand and therefore the look of a poem on the page when it is printed is not necessarily an indication of intent by the poet – it may be the *typography*. There are conventions in *typography* for poems which are adhered to by certain editions but ignored in others. For example, many of the pre-1900 poems start each line with a capital letter. This is of no significance – it is a typographical choice. Similarly, whether lines are indented or blocked may be typographical, rather than meaningful. Similarly, line length is often a feature of *metre*. Check that a line is, in fact, "longer" metrically before commenting on it. You should always look for other, supporting, evidence if you are going to make any link between layout on the page and meaning.

Capitalisation of individual words in a poem may be deliberate. Pre-1900 poets often capitalised virtues, as in Truth, Beauty, Purity or Nature. You should be able to tell whether capitalisation is a printing convention, or for a purpose, from the context. Where this is critical to understanding, it has been mentioned in the commentaries.

You will see in the older poems that the final *"-ed"* of the past tense of verbs may be depicted as *"'d"*, as in *"reap'd"* or *"drows'd"* in *"To Autumn"* by Keats. This is simply to indicate that the words should be pronounced as one syllable, rather than two. Sometimes, to make a full metric line, they would have been pronounced as two: *"rea-ped"*, *"drow-sed"*. Alternatively, words which are usually pronounced as a single syllable were sometimes elongated to two, to complete a metric line. This was indicated by an accent symbol above the second syllable. So, *"barréd"*, line 25, has an accent on *"barréd"*, as it would have been pronounced as two syllables *"bar-red"* to complete the metric line.

Preparing for the Unseen Poems

The best preparation for this component of the examination is to read, and listen to, poetry of all kinds, regularly. There are websites which will deliver a *"poem-a-day"* to your mobile. These two combine contemporary American poetry with classics:

https://www.poets.org/poetsorg/poem-day

https://www.poetryfoundation.org/newsletter

The Poetry Foundation website enables you to browse poems clustered by theme. This is a particularly useful feature to enable you to practise comparing poems.

How to use this Guide

As the modern poems within the anthology are copyrighted to the authors, it has not been possible to print them within this Guide. You will therefore need to read the commentaries with a copy of the text alongside. However, the poems have been quoted in places for illustrative purposes. Where the poems are out of copyright, they have been quoted at greater length.

Bibliography

Edexcel have published supporting materials for the Collection which are available to teachers.

Further reading on context can be found on the following useful websites:

http://www.bl.uk

The British Library has a number of articles in their Discovery section on the Romantics and on modern literature.

Many of the modern poets have their own websites, which are worth exploring for autobiographical details and commentaries on their poems.

The Poems

Introduction to the Romantic Poets

There is one thing that *any fule kno*[6] about the "Big Five" Romantic poets: they died in reverse order of being born. So, Wordsworth (1770-1850), Coleridge (1772-1834), Byron (1788-1824) Shelley (1792-1822), Keats (1795-1821). The mystic William Blake (1757-1827) is also part of this Movement.

The Romantic movement, or Romanticism, was a reaction to the preceding Age of Enlightenment, which valued rational, scientific thought above the revelation of emotions, the imagination, and the transforming power of the natural world. Wordsworth, in his preface to *"The Lyrical Ballads"* (1798), which he co-authored with Coleridge, described poetry as the *"spontaneous overflow of powerful feelings"*. Romantic Poetry is characterised by a *focus on the sensibilities:* a recognition of the *"sublime"* in the natural world; a willingness to engage in the imaginative possibilities of a supernatural world which co-exists with ours; the expression of intense emotions; a questioning of the nature of Art and aesthetics and the creative process; an exploration of spirituality, religious beliefs and the meaning of life.

Romantic poets were also anxious to break away from the rigid rules of *poesy*, such as the strict use of rhythm and rhyme, exhibited by earlier poets such as Alexander

---

[6] Molesworth in *"Down with Skool"* (sic), G. Willans. 1953.

Pope (1688-1744), seeking for a more natural rhythm, closer to speech, and a more colloquial *lexis*.[7] Perhaps the most notable difference between the earlier, Augustine poets such as Dryden and Pope is in the much less frequent use of *end-stopping* where the end of the metric line rhymes and completes the meaning of a clause or sentence. The opposite of this is *enjambment*, where the sense runs over one line and onto the next. However, many of the Romantics' earlier poems are written in prescribed forms – such as *sonnets* – and their poems often do have a regular rhythm and a regular rhyme scheme.

The poets were also revolutionary in their support for the overthrow of the established order through non-violent protest and championed the plight of the working poor. This is particularly evident in Blake's *"London"*.

Keats, Wordsworth and Blake are represented in this Collection. The more modern poets included share characteristics with them, particularly in their **evocation of the natural world, the landscape and the weather**.

---

[7] *Lexis* is vocabulary

To Autumn – John Keats

Context

In his tragically short life, Keats (1795-1821), who died of tuberculosis at age 25, produced poetry which, by the 20th century, had come to be considered some of the greatest in the English language. His first volume of poetry was produced in 1817, when he was only 22. The full title of the poem is *"Ode: To Autumn"* and it is the last in a series of six *Odes*, written in 1819, and his last major work.

This poem illustrates the Romantic poets' urge to express intense emotions and their belief in the healing powers of Nature on the spirit of Man.

Themes

The poem is a lush **description of Autumn**, a time of ripeness and fulfilment. It is frequently associated in poetry with the middle years of a person's life, when the youthful innocence of Spring and the full-flowering of Summer have past, but before the onset of old age in Winter. It is perhaps ironic that Keats should have chosen this season to celebrate, as he died before he reached his own middle-age.

The Romantics believed that mankind was linked spiritually to the natural world and that the power of Nature was restorative of the human spirit. Browning's *"Home Thoughts…"*, and Thomas's *"Adlestrop"* both explore **the restorative power of nature**.

The poem is remarkable both for its detailed observations of nature and the sensuous imagery with which it is described. In the use of **sensuous imagery**, the poem can be compared with Afrika's *"Nothing's Changed"* which uses similar poetic techniques. It can be contrasted with the harsher tones of Blake's description of *"London"*, where detailed description is minimal.

Form, structure and language

An *ode* is a lyric (rather than *narrative*[8]) poem which often talks to (*addresses*[9]) or celebrates an object, person or place. The inspiration found in writing the poem leads to a deeper understanding, or *revelation*, of the meaning of an important event in the poet's life or on the meaning of life in general.

The structure of Romantic Odes varies. Keats has chosen three stanzas of eleven lines, each with a regular rhyme scheme: *abab cde dcce* (stanza one) or *abab cde cdde* (stanzas two and three). He also uses an underlying metre of *iambic pentametre*, although there is considerable variation across the stanzas. *Autumn* is a time of completion and ripeness, of settled weather and quiet sounds. The regular, tight structure gives the poem a feeling of stillness and fulness, in keeping with the subject matter.

---

[8] A *narrative* poem is one that tells a story over time. A *lyric* poem tends to focus on a single event, emotion or person at one moment in time.
[9] Also called *apostrophe*

The **first stanza** opens with an address, or *apostrophe,* to Autumn, describing it as a *"season of mists"* and a time of calm when nature is delivering the fruits of summer (*"mellow fruitfulness"*). Autumn is also bathed in sunlight, even though the sun is now lower in the sky and closer to earth (*"bosom-friend"*) than it was in summer, and less powerful (*"the maturing sun"*). The sun and Autumn work closely together (*"conspiring"*) to produce the fruits of the harvest season – the grapes on the vines; the apples on the trees, so heavy they *"bend"* the branches; the pumpkins and other *"gourds"*; the ripe nuts; the late-blooming flowers that provide the bees with even more honey than they could store in Summer.

The preponderance of *"s"* and *"m"* sounds gives the whole stanza a hypnotic, trance-like tone. Keats uses a *semantic field*[10] of fullness and bounty: *"load", "bend", "ripeness", "swell", "plump", "budding", "o'erbrimm'd"*. Notice also how the repetition of *"budding more/And still more"*, spills across lines 8 and 9, like the flowers. The last line with the repeated *"mmm"* sounds in *"summer"*, *"o'erbrimm'd"* and *"clammy"* is *onomatopoeic*[11], like the murmuring of bees. Finally, the stanza ends on another sensuous image – the contrasting cool and damp of the inside of the bee's hives: *"clammy cells"*.

---

[10] A *"semantic field"* is a group of words associated with a particular topic.
[11] *Onomatopoeia* is the technique of using words that reproduce sounds.

In **stanza two**, *Autumn* is *personified* as a woman bringing in the harvest. The series of images place the harvest scene at a time when harvesting would have been done largely by hand, before the Industrial Revolution replaced men with farm machines, a process that was accelerating during Keats' lifetime.

The stanza opens with a *rhetorical question* to the reader, including us in the poet's vision of *Autumn* sitting in her "*store*", where the harvest will be gathered in. He imagines *Autumn* as a woman sitting on the floor of this storeroom ("*granary*") as a soft breeze moves her hair. The wind is "*winnowing*" because "*to winnow*" is to separate the grain from the ears of corn ("*chaff*") of a wheatsheaf by throwing it up into the wind. He then imagines her asleep in a field, overcome with the smell of the poppies that grow among the corn. Poppies are symbols of sleep, as some species produce opium, a powerful narcotic. She has only managed to reap part of the field ("*half-reap'd furrow*"), so the remainder of the corn and flowers, which are tangled together ("*twinéd flowers*"), are spared from her scythe ("*hook*"). The next vision of her is as a woman who goes behind the men who cut the corn to collect the grain that has fallen to the ground ("*gleaner*"), filling her bags and carrying them back on her head ("*laden head*") to bring them back to the barn. Lastly, he imagines her waiting patiently by a cider-press, watching the slow drip ("*oozing*") of the juice from the crushed apples into the barrels.

Stanza three opens with a further *rhetorical question*, looking back on the passing year. The *"songs of spring"* are bird songs, which are loudest in spring when they are establishing nesting territories and seeking mates. Keats urges *Autumn* to forget them – she has her own music. This music is soft, in tune with the *"mellow"* weather and softer light of the waning year. This music can be heard best in the evening under a "mackerel sky[12]" (*"barred clouds"*) which may bring a change of weather. For now, the sunset turns the fields pink (*"rosy hue"*) and the small sound of tiny insects (*"gnats"*) can be heard. They seem to be mourning for the dying year, as they float (*"borne aloft/or sinking"*) on the evening breeze. Notice how Keats uses the *enjambment* of lines 28 to 29 to replicate the gnats' movement – ending the line up in the air on *"aloft"* and dropping onto *"Or sinking"*. The sound of insects is joined by lambs bleating, *"hedge-crickets"* (similar to grasshoppers) chirping, and the soft calls of a robin, (*"redbreast"*) whose song in autumn is much quieter than in summer. Finally, the waning of the year and approach of winter is seen in the *"gathering swallows"*, who twitter as they prepare for their migration back to their winter homes in the south.

---

[12] A *"mackerel sky"* is a term to describe a sky which precedes a low-pressure front, often bringing rain. See a picture here: https://en.wikipedia.org/wiki/File:Mackerelskylincolnshire.jpg

Composed Upon Westminster Bridge , September 3, 1802 – William Wordsworth

Context

Wordsworth lived most of his life in the countryside of the Lake District, so a visit to London was an uncommon occurrence. The incident that inspired this poem was a coach trip made with his sister, Dorothy, through London on his way to Dover. Dorothy described the scene from the bridge in her journal: *"the houses not overhung by their clouds of smoke, and were spread out endlessly; yet the sun shone so brightly, with such a pure light, that there was something like the purity of one of Nature's own grand spectacles."*

The Romantics took themselves seriously as men who, through their poetry, could help others understand the world around them. The creative process and the workings of the imagination were worth exploration in themselves, giving us an insight into our relationship to the physical world around us (loosely defined as "Nature") and how we might tap into powers beyond the merely physical. In another age, this could be equated with "religion", but the Romantics were, primarily, atheists and did not equate this awareness of spirituality with any established religion.

Themes

The poem is written **in praise of London**, much as Keats' poem praises "*Autumn*". Wordsworth's response to the sight of London in the fresh, morning air is a spiritual cleansing and sense of a "*calm so deep*". **Joy in a moment in time and the spirit of place** is also celebrated in Thomas's "*Adelstrop*" and in Browning's memories of England in "*Home Thoughts from Abroad*" Arguably, it is also present in Davidson's "*In Romney Marsh*", although there is less emotional intensity.

Wordsworth's description of London can be compared to William Blake's, who lived in London and saw it very differently. At the close of the 18th century, London was beginning to experience the effects of the Industrial Revolution, with a rapidly rising population, increasing poverty, and inadequate housing and sanitation. In contrast to the "*smokeless air*", Blake's London is one that needs chimney sweeps to clean the chimneys which belch coal-smoke into the sooty air, "*black'ning*" the buildings.

Form, structure and language

"*Westminster Bridge*" is a Petrarchan *sonnet*. Petrarch was a Renaissance Italian poet after whom the Italian form of the 14-line poem known as a *sonnet* was named, although it was not invented by him. *Sonnets* are not always about love. They are often used to make an argument, or put forward a proposition, or idea, which is then explored, and an answer, or response, supplied.

In the traditional *sonnet* form, the proposition occurs within the first eight lines (the *octet*) and is answered in the next six lines (the *sestet*). At line 9 there is a *volta*, or turn, where the proposition turns to response. The rhyme scheme in a Petrarchan *sonnet* is *abbaabba cdcdcd*. However, there are many variations of the *sonnet* form, such as the English (or Shakespearian), Miltonian or Keatsian, where the rhyme scheme and positioning of the *volta* are variable.

The underlying *metre* is *iambic pentametre*, but with considerable variation.

Wordsworth opens his *sonnet* with a proposition – that there is nothing more beautiful on earth than the sight of London in the early morning, as viewed from Westminster Bridge. A person who is not "touched" by this sight must lack spirituality ("*dull ...of soul*"). The City is *personified* as a woman wearing the dawn as a "*garment*". Notice the use of *enjambment* between lines 4 and 5, which puts emphasis on "*the beauty*". Looking along the Thames, as he heads for the old Dover Road out of London, Wordsworth uses an "*asyndetic*[13]" list to build the cityscape before him. This

---

[13] "*asyndetic*" lists use commas to separate the elements of the list; "*syndetic*" lists use conjunctions, such as "*and*".

was before the Houses of Parliament and Big Ben, which now dominate the view from Westminster Bridge, were built, but some landmarks would be recognisable today, such as the buildings of Middle Temple, one of the Inns of Court, and the dome of St Paul's Cathedral. The *"theatres"* were probably Vauxhall and Astley's Amphitheatre, now demolished. The *"ships"* would have filled the Thames, as London was a major port. This view lies *"open to the fields"* as Westminster was still a semi-rural area in the early 19th century.

The description of the view ends with the last line of the *octet*. *"bright and glittering"* is the sun reflecting off the buildings in air that is *"smokeless"* because it is early morning. When the coal-burning factories and domestic fires start up, the air will become thick with soot, resembling Blake's *London*.

The *volta* occurs at line 9, where Wordsworth begins to compare his view of London with the Lake District. He seems surprised that an urban cityscape can compare favourably with the countryside with which he is familiar. He exclaims that *"Never"* did the rising sun cover the landscape of the Lake District *"more beautifully"* and that the peacefulness of the city soothes his soul as effectively (*"a calm so deep!"*). He sees the Thames flowing freely through the middle of the city. The Thames was much wider and stretched further inland, to the Strand, before the Victoria

Embankment was built in the mid-1800s. Compare this to Blake's image of the *"charter'd Thames"*, a river which is bound by warehousing and commercial activity. He returns to his *personification* of the city in the final line, listening for her *"heart"* and finding that it has slowed to stillness. His surprise at the peace that lies on the city is shown by the exclamation *"Dear God!"* and the exclamation marks after *"deep!"* and the final *"still!"* The sight is transcendent – lifting him to a higher plane of awareness and linking him to the natural world.

London – William Blake

Context

Like other Romantics, Blake challenges the supremacy of rational, scientific thought, seeking for spirituality and the transforming power of the imagination in human lives. He was a visionary and mystic, as well as a painter and engraver. Much of his poetry is the poetry of "*radical protest*"[14], championing the plight of the urban poor. Prior to the "Industrial Revolution", Britain was largely an agrarian economy – one based on the production of materials from the countryside, primarily food and wool. "The Industrial Revolution" is the name given to the period between, roughly, the mid-18th century and the middle of the 19th century which shifted Britain from an economy based on agriculture to one based on manufacturing. It was made possible by a series of inventions and developments in, particularly, textiles, steam power and iron making. Taken together, these inventions and developments in engineering replaced the cottage industries and led to a move of the majority of the population away from the countryside into the towns where the new factories were often sited. By 1851, half the population of Britain lived in towns. This shift led to considerable social challenges, including pressure on housing, sanitation and water provision. It also required changes to traditional working patterns which, in a rural environment (largely

---

[14] Peter Ackroyd at
http://www.bbc.co.uk/arts/romantics/intro.shtml

determined by the cycle of day and night and the seasons) had been the norm, but, in an industrial setting, imposed terrible hardships on men, women and children – long hours without respite, seven days a week working and children working in mines and factories at a very young age.

Blake was born and lived in London all his life. The poem *"London"* is taken from the collection *"Songs of Experience"* (1794), a counterpart to *"Songs of Innocence"* (1789), which Blake describes on the cover of the combined volume as *"the two contrary states of the human soul"*. Childhood, for the Romantics, was a time of innocence, in that it was unconstrained by the conventions of society and the stifling authority of Church and State. *"Experience"* is the exposure to these corrupting influences, against which Blake protests. The poem is a condemnation of a ruling class that ignores the plight of the urban poor and is blind to the hardships caused by the Government's failure to respond to societal change. *"London"* is its corrupt capital.

Themes

In *"London"*, Blake explores the *symbiosis*[15] between people and place, as does Wordsworth in *"On Westminster Bridge"*. Both poems show the **links between people and the places they live**, each bound

---

[15] *Symbiosis* means the interdependence of living things, each dependent on the other.

to the other. Where Wordsworth sees the city as uplifting, Blake sees it as corrupt and corrupting, polluting the lives of those that live within it. Fleur Adcock also explores how a place can affect the emotional well-being of people, as she rejects *Stewart Island* with its deceitful appearance.

"*London*", "*Westminster Bridge*", "*Adelstrop*" and "*Nothing's Changed*" all strongly evoke **a particular place at a particular time**.

Form, Structure and Language

In keeping with the title of his two collections, many of Blake's poems are written in simple, song-like rhythms with much repetition. The *metre* is regular *iambic tetrametre* (four stresses in a line of *iambs* – ti-**TUM**) and has a regular *abab* rhyme scheme. Much of the poem's effectiveness lies in the contrast between this sing-song form and the serious subject matter, the repetition hammering home the message of lives robbed of the uplifting power of imagination and spirit, because they are impoverished by the oppression of the State, Commerce and the Church.

The **opening stanza** places the poet in the streets of London, the word "*wander*" suggesting familiarity with his surroundings and the universality of the sights and sounds around him – he does not have to search them out. "*Chartered*" means here "*managed for profit*", as a "charter" was a licence to trade. Not only are the streets he walks through bound to the "profit motive", but even the natural flow of the River Thames has become bound and confined by the same motive; the Thames was a major shipping route, bringing goods and raw materials, particularly coal, from the Pool of London in the east, and was bounded by wharves and warehouses on both banks.

As he *"wanders"*, Blake notes the faces of the people he passes, which seem to bear signs of frailty and sorrow. Note how Blake changes the regular *iambic* rhythm here to emphasise the word *"Marks"*. He *inverts* (turns around) the ti-**Tum** of the *iamb* to create a *trochee* (**Tum**-ti):

*"**Marks** of /**weak**ness/, **marks** of/ **woe**"*

This line is called a *trochaic tetrametre* – three full feet of *trochees* plus one incomplete foot - or *catalexis*[16]. This is the rhythm of Blake's most famous poem *"The Tyger"*:

Tyg**er/, **tyg**er,/ **burn**ing/ **bright
In** the **for**ests **of** the **night

Stanza 2, with the repeated *"every"*, continues the idea of ubiquity – no-one in this city is free from the blight. *"Every man"* is probably also to be read as "Everyman", the eponymous hero of the medieval morality play that follows the journey of an ordinary man through his life. The stanza depicts the sounds of woe as the people cry out in their pain. *"Every ban"* is most likely to be a

---

[16] A *catalectic* line is one that has an incomplete *metric foot* at the end.

reference to the notices read out in church before a marriage, as in *"reading the ban(n)s"*, which would reflect Blake's own views on the institution of marriage and foreshadows the last lines of the poem. They are bound to a life which imprisons them, both body and soul. The *"mind-forged manacles"* are a *metaphor* for the suppression of the imagination and spirit of people who are trapped in this corrupt society and its conventions.

Stanza 3 moves from the general to the specific – giving examples of the cries of the *"Every man"* of the previous stanza. First, the cry of the child chimney-sweep is heard. Fires in London were fuelled by coal, which leaves a dense black soot, requiring regular brushing to avoid chimney fires. Small boys were sent up the chimneys to sweep them out, a dangerous, and at times fatal occupation. Their plight was made famous in the book *"The Water Babies"* (1863) by Charles Kingsley, which Blake anticipated by some years. The *"black'ning church"* is a comment on the attitude of the church towards this horror. It is *"black'ning"*, as all buildings in London did, from the soot deposits, and should be protesting against the toll taken on the sweeps. The next image is of a soldier dying for his country. The soldier is *"hapless"* as he has no choice whether to fight or not. His *"sigh"* is both a cry of helplessness and his dying breath. This is an example of how Blake moves from the literal (a sighing soldier) to the visionary – the sigh becomes an image of blood on the walls. In this stanza, Blake is making an ironic comment on a society which allows this to happen. Both institutions, Church and Crown/State, are complicit in the pain of the oppressed.

In **Stanza 4**, Blake reserves his harshest criticism for the institution of marriage. Blake believed in a God, or supreme being, but was deeply critical of the Church as an organisation, seeing it as an instrument for the suppression of individual liberty and freedom of thought. He saw the institution of marriage as a shackling of man's nature and instincts, particularly in the elevation of Chastity and Marriage as virtues in themselves, regardless of how men and women felt about their relationships with one another. As he wanders through the streets at night, he hears the cries of the young prostitutes, of whom there were many thousands in London, although it is not clear that all were what we would call "prostitutes" today. This term was also applied to unmarried women living with men, or unmarried mothers. The plight of unmarried mothers was particularly harsh, and Blake imagines how their instinct to soothe their child when it cries is transformed into a "*curse*" as they regret having given birth. He then expands this vision to show how the fate of these poor unfortunates is bound up with the lives of the "respectable marrieds". Instead of a "carriage", the newly-weds travel in a "*hearse*" – a vehicle for carrying coffins. This is a comment on, first, the deadening institution of marriage, which at the time, was often arranged or subject to strict societal conventions, which might not reflect the desires of the couple. Second, and more sinisterly, "*plagues*" is a reference to sexually transmitted infections, commonly gonorrhoea or the

deadly syphilis, transmitted by these "prostitutes".
Unmarried men visited prostitutes because respectable
unmarried women were expected to remain "chaste"
until marriage. The men contracted a STI which they
then passed to their wives, which, with few effective
treatments, resulted in infertility in the woman, or
death.

This is a bleak, apocalyptic view of a society which
blights the lives of its citizens, with London as its source
and symbol.

I Started Early – Took My Dog – Emily Dickinson

Context

Emily Dickinson (1830-1886) was an American poet who spent most of her adult life in seclusion in the town of Amherst, Massachusetts, where she was born. Her father was a lawyer and trustee of Amherst College, a private liberal arts college which had been founded by her grandfather. She was well-educated, attending school until the age of seventeen, although she gave up attending College in her first year.

Although she was a prolific poet – she wrote almost 1800 poems – few were published in her lifetime and early versions of her work were much altered by the family before publication. It was not until 1955 that a definitive collection became available.

Themes

The poem is a highly imaginative, dream-like account of a walk by the sea, in which Dickinson imagines *"the Tide"* trying to overwhelm her. The place of the walk is generalised, as is the time; the focus is on her realisation of the **size and power of the Sea**, and more generally, **Nature**, comparing herself to a *"Mouse"* on the shore, or a *"Dew"*-drop on a leaf. This **generalised view of Place** can be compared with Fanthorpe's *"First Flight"* and contrasted with the specific descriptions of *London* made by both Wordsworth and Blake. In *"Nothing's Changed"*, Afrika also takes a walk through a familiar place and his forensic, sensuous description of the terrain can be contrasted with Dickinson's use of fantastical imagery.

Form, language and structure

Dickinson's poems were hand-written, and her penmanship is individual and eccentric, particularly in her use of capitalisation and frequent use of hyphens. Whether the use of these features in an individual poem is for effect, or merely a stylistic choice applied to her writings more generally (she used the same notation in her prose writings) is difficult to determine. There are many academic papers written which attempt to analyse Dickinson's usage of these features. In "*I Started Early – Took My Dog*", one of her most famous poems[17], there are frequent hyphens, which could appear to be random, but also replace conventional commas and full stops. Nearly every noun and noun-phrase is capitalised, which, in the era of text messaging, tends to make us see emphasis ("shouty caps") where none may be intended. Some suggestions on the effect of these notations are given in this commentary, but much is dependent on the reader's interpretation.

Dickinson most often writes in *common metre,* with *quatrains*[18] of alternating lines of *iambic tetrametre* and *iambic trimetre.*[19] Her rhyme scheme here is *xaxa,* as in

---

[17] The line is often quoted and is the title of a 2010 novel by Kate Atkinson.
[18] *Quatrains* are four-line stanzas

ballads, where the *x* denotes a non-rhyme and *a* denotes a rhyming line. *Ballads* are typically narrative poems, as here, where Dickinson gives a fantastical account of an encounter with The Tide, which is *personified* as a god-like Man. The fantastical elements and the eroticism this poem make it seem surprisingly modern. The sexual elements are one reason why her work was censored by early editors.

The **first stanza** starts with the declaration of the poet's intent to go for a walk to the sea in the early morning with her dog, Carlo, a Newfoundland that was her companion for sixteen years. The poem quickly becomes a dream-like fantasy, as the Sea seems to be imagined as a gigantic building. From the *"basement"*/bottom of the Sea she imagines Mermaids surfacing to look at her.

Here she creates a sing-song rhythm as her capitalisation loosely follows the *iambic* metre: "**Ear**ly", "the **Sea**", "The **Mer**maids", "the **Base**ment". However, lack of capitalisation also brings extra emphasis to certain words, as in *"And visited the **Sea**".*

In the **second stanza**, she moves from the idea of a *"Basement"* to an *"Upper Floor"*, like the swell of waves from trough to crest. *Frigate* birds (large black and white seabirds) flying on the crest of the waves try to catch her. *"Hempen"* means made from hemp, a fibrous plant, from which ropes are made, extending

---

[19] Alternating lines with 4 and 3 heavy beats in the pattern *ti-**TUM** (iambs): I **star**/ted **Ear**/ly – **Took**/ my **Dog** - /*

the nautical theme. She compares the tough, twisted rope to the birds' claws reaching for her; because she looks so small, alone on the *"Sands"*, they think she is prey – a *"Mouse"*.

Stanza three opens with another declaration: *"But no Man moved Me..."*. The use of *"But"* seems to contrast the gaze of the *Mermaids* and the attack of the *Frigate* birds as a different quality of experience from the attentions of a *Man*. However, the approaching *"Tide"*, as it moves up the beach to where she stands, is *personified* as a man who makes sexual advances. First, he touches her *"Shoe"*, moves up to the *"Apron"* over her skirt, up to the *"Belt"* on her waist, and then up to her *"Bodice"*, over her breasts. Notice how each part of her clothing is capitalised, marking out his relentless approach. Notice also the isolation of *"-too-"* between the two hyphens for isolation, as if to show her shock at his advances.

In the **fourth stanza**, the lecherous nature of this *"Man"* is evident from the common *metaphor* of him wanting to *"eat me up"* and the word *"wholly"*, suggesting possession. However, she does not seem frightened by this possibility, describing his desire in a delicate *simile,* comparing herself to a *"Dew"*-drop on a *"Dandelion"* leaf (*"Sleeve"*) which he will easily lap up. She seems to be hypnotised by his approach, as she is startled into movement and tries to escape up the beach.

In **stanza five**, the personification of the Sea as *"He"* continues, his relentless advances and her helplessness shown by the repeated *"And He – He followed – close* *behind* – " The Tide chases her up the beach, the frothy bubbles as the waves advance (*"Silver Heel"*) lapping at her *"Ankle"* and then flowing over her *"Shoes"*. The imagery of the silvery water continues with the word *"Pearl"*.

In **stanza six**, the waters follow her until they reach the barrier of the *"Solid Town"*, where the Tide is stopped. He is not welcome here. She imagines the Sea bowing to her, as if acknowledging his defeat, before withdrawing down the beach.

The poem is a sexual fantasy , where the woman is both fascinated and excited by the relentless advances of the male figure. However, the social conventions of the time demand that she reject his advances, seeking the safety of the *"Solid Town"*, a symbol of conventional, Victorian morality.

Where the Picnic Was – Thomas Hardy

Context

Thomas Hardy (1840-1928) is probably better known for his novels than for his poetry. He wrote poems in his youth but did not return to poetry until the completion of his last novel, "*Jude the Obscure*", in 1895. His novels, particularly "*Tess of the D'Urbervilles*" and "*Jude the Obscure*", are acknowledged as some of the best novels of the Victorian era, challenging Victorian bourgeois values, exploring the plight of women and sexual hypocrisy, and the effects of the Industrial Revolution on the rural poor.

Hardy's relationships with women were problematical. He had several disappointing romantic relationships as a young man. His first marriage, to Emma Gifford, ended unhappily after a long separation, although he was devastated by her death and she is the focus of this poem, which was written in 1913, a year after her death. He was for some years enamoured of a married woman who would not have an affair with him but remained a life-long friend and correspondent. In his later life, he was infatuated with a succession of much younger women. Two years after his first wife's death, he remarried, but the marriage was not happy.

Themes

The poem is *elegiac*[20] – it recalls a happier time, when Hardy, his wife and friends enjoyed a picnic. Like others in the collection, it shows the close **relationship between place and memory** and how places enable us to recall emotions first experienced there. Similarly, powerful emotions are recalled by Afrika in *"Nothing's Changed"* when he returns to the place where he grew up and Jennings' *"Absence"* where she recalls a lost love. It is also a reflection on **Time Past**, **Change, and Loss**. Many poets use summer as an image of happier times, with change and loss symbolised by a change in the season to autumn or winter.

Form, Language and Structure

Hardy's negative, sad mood is reflected in the leaden, two-stress *metre* (*"dimetre"*) of the verse form, like the weighty tread of coffin-bearers walking in two-time: "*of* **branch** *and* **briar**/*on the* **hill** *to the* **sea**/*I* **slow**ly **climb**/...". The rhyme scheme is irregular but uses a limited range of rhymes. The first two stanzas of nine lines rhyme: *abacbaddc, ababccddb*. The third, twelve-line stanza extends the pattern: *aabbccdefdef*, like a truncated *sonnet*.

In **stanza one**, Hardy revisits the place where he enjoyed a picnic with his wife and two friends. The poem is written in the present tense, thus giving it immediacy, as if we are walking alongside him. The picnic was in summer, when they *"made a fire"*,

---

[20] Like an *elegy* – a song of mourning for the dead

collecting branches from round about. Now it is winter, and his change of mood is evident from the way he "*slowly climb[s]*" through the mud ("*mire*"). He looks over the deserted scene, recalling the time they spent together ("*scan and trace*") and mourning time lost.

In **stanza two**, Hardy implies the contrast with the summer weather with the description of the "*cold wind*" and "*grey sea*". The place of the fire is still clearly visible from the "*burnt circle*", an image of the broken circle of friendship. Like the "*stick-ends*", no longer complete, he is the only thing left ("*last relic*") of the little group of friends who came up the hill for a pleasant day out.

In **stanza three**, Hardy tells us that this is an annual pilgrimage – he has come "*just as last year*". The smell of the sea ("*brine*") stretching to the horizon ("*strange straight line*") is the same as in the happier time. In the seventh line of the stanza (line 25), Hardy reveals that the reason for his melancholy is not just the change of season from summer to winter, but the loss of two of his companions from that day – two have moved from the Dorset countryside to the city ("*urban roar*") where there are "*no picnics*" and the other (his wife) has died ("*shut her eyes/For evermore*").

Hardy shows how, although the physical characteristics of a Place may remain unchanged – the climb up the hill, the smell, the view – his response to it is bound up with memories and feelings. Similarly, Wordsworth's and Blake's views of London are dependent on their emotional responses to it, not the physical landscape. Jennings in "*Absences*" recognises that the garden is unchanged physically, but it is changed utterly by her feelings of loss. On the other hand, whilst the physical landscape has changed utterly in Afrika's "*Nothing's Changed*", his feelings have not, and he overlays what he hears and sees with these powerful feelings of anger. Similarly, Adcock sees deceit and lies in "*Stewart Island*", as her feelings about New Zealand are already negative and she has "*decided to leave*".

Adlestrop – Edward Thomas

Context

Edward Thomas (1878-1917) was a British writer and poet who was killed in action in the First World War. He was encouraged to write poetry by the American poet Robert Frost, with whom he had a close friendship whilst the latter lived in England. Thomas is one of the so-called "Georgian poets" who were writing during the early part of the reign of George V, and whose work was published in four volumes of the same name between 1912 and 1922. The anthologies included other "War poets", such as Rupert Brooke and Siegfried Sassoon. The Georgian poets have been characterised as producing lyric poetry on themes of nature and the countryside, often in traditional forms. Many of the poems are now considered weak and lacking in originality. However, "*Adelstrop*" regularly features in lists of the nation's favourite poems.

Adelstrop, in Gloucestershire, was a station on the Cotswold line which closed in 1966 under the infamous Beeching cuts to railway services. All traces of the stop, except the name board and a bench, have now disappeared. Thomas stopped there in June, 1914, on his way to visit Robert Frost in Ledbury, Herefordshire. The poem was written a few months before Thomas's death three years later at the Battle of Arras in 1917 but not published until afterwards. This knowledge gives an added poignancy to the poem, as Thomas recalls, and bids farewell to, the peace and tranquillity of England that will be shattered forever.

Themes

This lyric poem **freezes a moment in Time and Place.** It can be compared with Wordsworth's *"On Westminster Bridge"* when he looks at London in the early morning light. Whereas Wordsworth details the urban landscape– *"ships, towers, domes,"* – Thomas records the rural features before him – *"willow, willowherb, and grass,"* to particularise the scene. Both poems express an intense emotional response triggered by a unique moment in time in a unique place. Browning's poem, *"Home Thoughts..."* also conveys this moment of unexpected joy, when he is caught *"unaware"* (line 4). Both poems are revelatory - the beauty of the scene before them, and their response to it, is sudden and unexpected. There is a sense of wonder as the world around them reveals itself.

Form, structure and language

The poem is written in four *quatrains* with a regular rhyme scheme *xaxa,* where *x* is an unrhymed line. The underlying metre is *iambic tetrametre*, but with considerable variation[21]. Within this structure, Thomas creates a conversational tone by the frequent use of *enjambment* and *caesura*, creating the sense of long lines.

The conversational tone is established in the first line of **the first stanza**, with the affirmative *"Yes"*, as if he is responding to a question from a listener. He remembers

---

[21] This is sometimes called *long metre*.

only "*the name*" as he did not leave the train. The train unexpectedly stops at the station ("*Unwontedly*") in the "*heat*" of "*late June*". Notice how Thomas uses *enjambment* between lines two and three to place a stress on "*heat*" and between lines three and four to stress "*Unwontedly*". It is the silence caused by the drowsy "*heat*" coupled with the unexpected stop that creates this special moment in time.

In **stanza two**, Thomas uses short sentences to detail the small sounds he hears in the stillness – the hissing of the steam train, someone clearing his throat – to show how distinct and separate each sound is. The repeated "*no-one*" in line six emphasises the stillness and emptiness, as does the adjective "*bare*". It is the name on the name board – *Adlestrop* – that is significant, fixing the memory. Thomas's vision moves outwards from the name board, the *enjambment* across the stanza carrying him from the station to the countryside: "*only the name/And willows...*"

In **stanza three**, Thomas uses a *syndetic list* with the word "*and*", as he looks out across the fields, making each feature of the countryside distinct and special. Compare this with Wordsworth's *asyndetic* listing of the view from the bridge. "*Willows*" are trees, probably growing around the station, and "*willow-herb*" is a tall, pink flower often found growing on cleared or burned ground and along railway sidings. No doubt Thomas chose it for the repetition of "*willow*", but also the simple extension of "*-herb*" which lengthens the word and moves us further out . The farther meadows are described by the sibilance of "*grass/meadowsweet/*

haycocks". "*Meadowsweet*" is a creamy-white, frothy flower that grows among long, meadow grass. These images of stillness, and the white flowers particularly, are likened to the high, small "*cloudlets*" floating above him. Note the *alliterated* "*l*" sounds of "*still/lonely/cloudlets*" which slow the lines.

Thomas delays to **the final stanza** the revelation that while he has been sitting quietly at the station, for "*that minute*", a blackbird has been singing "*close by*". The bird's song is picked up and echoed by "*all the birds*" across the countryside, suggesting that only now does Thomas become aware of their singing. The sounds draw Thomas even further afield, out into the neighbouring counties, and, by inference, across rural England, an England which he now knows will be utterly changed by the War.

Home Thoughts from Abroad - Robert Browning

Context

This is Browning's most famous lyric poem. In classical times, a lyric poem was originally a poem set to music played on a *lyre*, a form of small harp, but came to be applied to any (short) poem which has love as its theme or explores and expresses the thoughts and feelings of the poet. It is essentially *non-narrative*; there is no story being told. The poem shows Browning's debt to the Romantics – the poetic movement that immediately preceded the Victorians, of whom the main exponents were Wordsworth, Byron, Coleridge, Shelley and Keats. The central theme of their poetry is the transcendent power of Nature and the value and authenticity of human emotions and feelings in the face of an increasingly rational and scientific approach to the world. They are spiritual, but not religious. The detailed references to the observed world and the emotional response to nature are hallmarks of the Romantic approach.

Browning's poem was published in 1845 in *"Dramatic Romances and Lyrics"*, number VII in a series of pamphlets containing plays and poems under the collective title *"Bells and Pomegranates"* – a reference to the Bible in which Aaron (Moses's brother) is described as having a robe hemmed with ornaments of this shape. Browning explained his choice of this reference as: *"the hem of the robe of the high priest"* to *indicate "the mixture of music with discoursing, sound with sense, poetry with thought."*

Themes

Browning travelled to Italy for the first time in the late 1830s and again in the early 1840s. Despite the tone of the poem, which compares Italy unfavourably to England, Browning was very fond of Italy and he and his wife, the poet Elizabeth Barrett Browning, made their home there after their marriage, although they returned to England for family visits. The poem evokes the sights and sounds of the English countryside and is **infused with nostalgia** for the home they have left behind. In this, it is similar in tone to Thomas's *"Adlestrop"* with its sense of a lost Eden. It also expresses **the importance of place in forming identity**. It can be contrasted with Adcock's views on *"Stewart Island"*, which are distorted by her dislike of the country of her birth.

Form, structure and language

Browning uses an irregular metric pattern throughout the two stanzas. Note how this irregular metre is used to match the poet's emotions. In stanza one, the *octet* is in *trochaic trimetre* for the first three lines, but as the emotion grows and he warms to his subject, the lines lengthen to *tetrametre* and then *pentametre*. The exclamation that ends the stanza is a *dimetre*, as if his emotions have overwhelmed him and he cannot go on. The rhyme scheme is regular – *ababccdd* – which again matches his growing emotion, as the rhymes become more closely packed towards the end.

Note also the characteristic use of *enjambment* and *caesura*, as between lines three and four, to put emphasis on *"Sees"*, and between eleven and twelve to emphasise *"Leans"*.

In **stanza one**, the poem opens with an exclamation, as if the emotion of longing has spilled out of him spontaneously. The word *"there"* is odd – in fact, it is often misquoted as *"here"*. After all, it is April in Italy as well. So, a contrast is made immediately – April in Italy is of quite a different quality, almost not like April at all. He is, of course, comparing the more temperate climate of England with the Mediterranean climate of Italy, to the latter's disadvantage. In England, spring comes stealthily (*"unaware"*), the leaves appearing as if overnight on the elm-trees and the surrounding bushes and the chaffinch (a small, pink-breasted songbird) has begun singing. But their arrival is gentle, unlike the sudden onset of a Mediterranean summer. The *octet* ends on another exclamation, to show how he is overwhelmed by the memory of his homeland.

In **stanza two**, one thought leads to another, as May follows April, the subject of the next *octet,* his emotions conveyed by the repeated exclamation mark after *"swallows"*. The references here are to two birds, the whitethroat and swallow, which migrate to England in the spring to breed - another symbol of how England's seasons change. The opening two lines of the stanza form an incomplete sentence, as if his memories are tumbling from him uncontrolled.

In line 11, the poet asks us to *"Listen!"* to the sound of a thrush in his garden (*"**my** blossomed..."*). The scene is described in detail, as if recalling an actual event. The thrush is sitting at the end of a spray of the pear-tree, which is growing in a hedge (perhaps the boundary of his garden) and leaning over into the neighbouring field, where it drops its *"Blossoms and dewdrops"* onto the clover crop below. Browning uses the subordination of this long sentence, between *"Hark!"* and *"That's the wise thrush;"* to lead us through the image of the blossoming pear-tree in the hedge, up and out over the field to where the thrush perches on the out-flung branch. Compare this with the way Edward Thomas moves the "viewer" from the station and out across the English countryside.

Browning's observations are accurate – the song thrush (*turdus philomelus*) prefers to sing perched at the end of a branch. Its song is characterised by the repetition of notes and phrases. The thrush is *"wise"* because it repeats itself to make sure it doesn't forget its song - and so that we do not presume that it cannot reproduce the first, glorious outpouring (*"rapture"*).

The lines of this *octet* now lengthen to *iambic pentametre* as his vision of England expands. The rhyme scheme subtly alters, but remains regular, the rhyming couplets used for emphasis: *aabcbcdd*.

The recollections of an English spring continue in the final quatrain. The fields are white with a late *"hoar"*-frost. However, by midday it will have warmed up and burnt off the dew, or frost, and the buttercups will open. The bright yellow buttercups are described as a gift or *dowry* to children – from the sun, possibly, as they reflect its yellow light. A favourite game of children used to be to test if you "liked butter" by holding a buttercup under the chin to see if it reflected yellow. It usually does, as the inside of a buttercup petal is shiny and light reflective. The buttercup is compared with the exotic *"melon flower"*, which is also yellow and much larger than a buttercup. The melon is a member of the same botanical family as cucumbers and squash, but they do not grow naturally in England as it is too cold.

There is some xenophobia[22] here perhaps. The Colonial British (although Italy was never a colony) prided themselves on their restraint and order; they saw themselves as "civilising" the peoples they came into contact with. Browning dismisses the *"gaudy"* melon flower for being too exotic, too extravagant and showy, preferring the unassuming native wildflower of England. However, Browning was well-travelled and cosmopolitan, and, at this time, had little reason to love the "British Public"; the reaction to his poetry, and in particular the long poem *"Sordello"* published in 1840, was generally negative and was criticised for its

---

[22] Fear of foreigners

obscurity. This criticism effectively hampered his career for years - after 1844 he published very little until late in life, and many of the poems now recognised as being his greatest (apart from the epic *"The Ring and the Book"* (1869)) pre-date his marriage and emigration to Italy.

Lines from this poem have been referenced by many poets, showing its enduring, and endearing, influence over time. It ranked number 42 in the Nation's 100 Favourite Poems poll carried out by the BBC (*"My Last Duchess"*, also by Browning, was at 69); there is a song by the same name by Clifford T Ward published in the 1970s; a poem by the novelist John Buchan; Carol Anne Duffy, the poet Laureate, named her autobiographical collection of love poems *"Rapture"* and quotes the poem in her dedication; Thomas Hardy's *"The Darkling Thrush"* references it; Rupert Brooke, poet of the First World War, echoes its sentiments in *"The Soldier"*.

First Flight – U A Fanthorpe

Context

U. A. Fanthorpe (1929-2009) taught for many years at Cheltenham Ladies College, latterly as Head of English, but in her 40s she abandoned teaching and went to work a s a receptionist in a psychiatric hospital. It was then she started writing poetry, publishing her first volume at the age of 50. Commenting on her late flowering as a poet she said: *"At once I'd found the subject that I'd been looking for all my life: the strangeness of other people, particularly neurological patients, and how it felt to be them, and to use their words."*

Her liking for using the words of others is evident in this poem, as it is a *dialogue* between two people – one, the poet as first-time flyer, and the other a frequent flyer who interrupts her thoughts with (unhelpful) comments and advice.

Themes

This poem sits oddly in a collection which focuses on memories of time and place which are often strongly rooted in a physical landscape. Here, we have a recollection of a first-time experience, in a generalised space (the cabin of an aircraft) and at no specific time. The focus here is on the emotions of the first speaker, as she grapples with the new sensation of being in flight and on how the world, and all that matters within it, is diminished by distance. **Ideas of "distance" and how it can change perceptions of time and place** are found

54

also in Browning's *"Home Thoughts…"*, where England becomes a lost Eden; in Alvi's *"Presents…"* where her homeland, Pakistan, becomes a mystical place but also one that symbolises the duality of her upbringing as an immigrant, and in Nicolson's *"Hurricane…"* where distance is bridged by a shared weather system. The poem can also be linked to Hannah's *"Postcards…"* which also explores **different attitudes to travelling**.

The typography and structure of the poem, opposing the two voices, contrasts their attitudes to the experience of travel - one full of wonder and "buoyed up", the other jaded and down to earth.

Form, structure and language

The two voices in the poem are indicated by standard and *italic* fonts. Although the poem is in *free verse,* many of the lines spoken by the first-time flyer have four stresses, giving a loose rhythm. The voice of the poet/first-time flyer consists mainly of couplets of short, incomplete sentences, as if thinking aloud. The experienced passenger makes short, declamatory statements, interspersed with rhetorical questions, to show his superior knowledge and experience.

In **couplet one,** she comments on the run-up to take off. She feels uncomfortable, as the movement is unnatural. The plane seems to lose its grip on the earth, creating a sliding sensation as caused by *"low tyre pressure"* on a car.

In **couplet two**, the plane takes off with a final burst of acceleration and banks as it climbs, the earth seemingly tilting below. She begins to comment on the actions of the "*experienced*" air-traveller – but is interrupted.

The interruption comes from (presumably) the man sitting next to her – one of the "*experienced*" – who comments, somewhat smugly, that this trip is only a short one ("*hop*") compared to others he has made. He perhaps senses her discomfort.

Lines 6 and 7 pick up the interrupted thought: "*The experienced solidly/Read Guardians...*". Most of her fellow travellers are businessmen, chatting about their offices and work: "*secretaries/Business lunches*". She is more concerned with trying to keep some contact with the land left behind, peering out of the aircraft window to try and see the last of ...

But her train of thought is again interrupted. The man explains that he is only doing this trip to tick it off a list: "*just to say I've done it.*" His casual attitude to flying is contrasted with her feelings of alienation from...

"*Familiar England*". Below her she can still see, in miniature, the features of the landscape around the airport. As the plane gains height, in a strange optical illusion, she sees an image of the sun ("*tiny-disc*")...**(lines 9 and 10)**

Again, her thoughts are interrupted by the man asking her to tell him when they are "*over water*". He cannot see out of the window, as he is on an aisle seat.

The tiny sun appears to "*run*" up the window. They are now in cloud, described by the *metaphor* of "*meringue*", indicating the white, fluffy appearance.

Her neighbour now informs her that they won't see water until they are over the Mediterranean. The abbreviation to "Med" shows his familiarity with the geography of the journey. His prosaic comment contrasts with her increased use of *figurative language*[23], showing their different responses to their shared experience.

In **lines 15 to 16,** she draws parallels between the effect of the orange light (of the sunset?) reflecting on the "*cumulus*" clouds and the same light spreading over the waves of the sea. Her sense of being already separated and distant from her starting place is conveyed in her use of the word "*home*", although she has travelled neither very far, nor for very long.

Her neighbour now gives her some practical advice about clothing. Where they are going has a temperate climate, neither cold (no "*overcoat*") nor hot ("*need a pullover*"). His rhetorical "*know what I mean?*" is intended to be helpful and friendly. But she is barely listening, caught up in thoughts about the meaning of her experience.

In **lines 20 to 23**, she expresses her feelings of disassociation from the world left behind. The past has become immaterial – all that matters now is what is to come ("*tomorrow*"). The forecasters – of weather, but also economic, political, social change – and lives lived by the clock have become meaningless. Time has no

---

[23] *Metaphor* and *simile*

meaning when you are far above the world; it changes as you travel from one place to another.

In **lines 23 – 26**, as if reacting to her continued silence, the man becomes more talkative, trying to impress her with his knowledge of the correct way to say *"Peking"*, which he has visited. *"Peking"* was an earlier romanisation[24] of the Chinese character for *"Beijing"*, the capital city of China. The pronunciation and spelling changed during Fanthorpe's lifetime, and there is a note of irony in her recollection of this conversation. As a teacher, it is highly unlikely that she would not have been fully aware of the shift. The man's comments are a further instance of his inability to see beyond the unimportant to the true significance of events. Her silence seems to provoke a hostile reaction, his sentences becoming short and imperative: *"Go on, say it."*

In the **last stanza,** she continues to ignore him. She feels increasingly detached from the real world left far below, expressed through the extravagant metaphor of the clouds looking like the full-bottomed wigs of high court judges, white and curly. A *"mackerel sky"* is a sky covered in clouds in a rippling, ribbon formation, patterned like the back of a mackerel fish. A judge's wig is made of tightly curled white horsehair similarly arranged in rows. Her idea is that, at this height, clouds rule the air – there is nothing over which Man can have

---

[24] A translation of an alphabet, such as Chinese ideograms (words represented as pictures) into letters used by the Romans, as in English and most other European languages.

authority. The idea of being now in the clouds' domain refers back to line 13, where she refers to *"meringue kingdom"*. Up here, life is unsustainable as it is *"too cold"*. Paradoxically, it is cold because *"too near the sun"* – above the clouds and atmosphere which trap the sun's heat and reflect it back to earth.

The strangeness of their situation is, of course, lost on her neighbour, who can only see their shared experience as transactional and mundane, rooted in useless facts. The insignificance of these two, little people in this alien environment is beyond his limited understanding.

Stewart Island – Fleur Adcock

Context

Fleur Adcock (born 1934) was born in New Zealand but spent most of her childhood in England. She returned to New Zealand as a teenager and then attended university in Auckland. On graduating, she became a librarian. Her time there was very unhappy. After two failed marriages, and the birth of two sons, she returned to England permanently in 1963. She was awarded the OBE for services to Literature in 1996.

Stewart Island is the third largest of the islands that make up New Zealand and lies 19 miles off the coast of South Island. Eighty percent of it is a nature reserve. It is renowned for its natural beauty and wildlife. The poem, written in 1971, recalls a visit made there by Adcock with her two sons.

Themes

Places reflect the feelings of the people that inhabit them. One person's Eden is another one's Hell. Whereas Wordsworth and Thomas use *Westminster Bridge* and *Adlestrop* to express feelings of wonder and delight, and Browning is filled with nostalgia for his homeland infusing it with beauty, Adcock's disillusion with her life is channelled into this account of her visit to the Island. It can be compared to Blake's "*London*", where Blake uses London as the focus for the injustices of his society, and to Hardy's "*Where the Picnic was*", where the place of pilgrimage reflects his feelings of sorrow and regret. Adcock suggests that *Stewart Island*

(and by extension New Zealand?) is a place of deceit –
picture postcard perfect but hiding a less pleasant
reality. The ideas of **deception and disappointment**
recur throughout.

Form, structure and language

Adcock has described her style: "*The tone I feel at home
in is one in which I can address people without
embarrassing them; I should like them to relax and
listen as if to an intimate conversation*"[25]. This tone of
intimacy is evident in this poem, in which we hear
Adcock's "voice". The single stanza of eighteen lines is
written in *free verse* with no rhyme. However, the short
lines are all roughly equal in length, with mainly four
stresses, potentially giving the poem a jaunty beat. By
making extensive use of *enjambment* and *caesura*,
carrying the sense of one line over to the next, Adcock
disrupts this rhythm and creates a conversational tone.
It is this that enables Adcock to make the poem both
darkly humorous, and bitingly sarcastic, as she
juxtaposes one idea against another, in succeeding
lines, in surprising ways:

*Fishermen with Scottish names (she
Ran off with one...)*

The first line is spoken by the "*hotel manager's wife*" to
Adcock, in response to Adcock wondering how the
woman can "*bear*" to live there. The word "*bear*"
immediately reveals Adcock's attitude to the place – she

---

[25] (*Strong Words*, Bloodaxe Books, 2000).

dislikes it. The woman's "*But...*" shows her surprise that anyone should ask such a question – beauty is, after all, why people visit the island. Adcock bluntly concedes the woman's point ("*True*") and starts to list some of its features: "*fine bay/all hills and atmosphere; white sand, and bush...*". The description is peculiarly generalised and impersonal – more like a picture on a postcard than a lived experience. Compare her description with the detailed, sensuous descriptions in both Wordsworth's and Thomas's poems. Adcock is detached, indifferent to the landscape, whereas Wordsworth and Thomas are bound up in an emotional and sensual response to what surrounds them.

Adcock acknowledges some human interest in the scene ("*oyster boats... Maori fishermen*") but then undercuts this with the revelation that the "*wife*" was, in fact, dissatisfied with her life and has "*run off*" with one of the fishermen. The reference to "*Scottish names*" suggests either that the indigenous Maori people have taken anglicised names or that most of them are now of mixed race. Either way, there is a suggestion of deceit, both by the "*wife*" and the "*fishermen*", which also reflects her feelings about the island. It looks pretty – but behind the façade there are lies.

This idea of the island hiding falsehoods continues in her description of her walk on the beach with her two sons. Positive and negative images alternate with each line. The water looks inviting, but it is "*too cold to swim*"; the sand holds treasure for the child, in the form of "*seashells*", but is infested with "*sandflies*"; her child's paddling is spoilt by when he is divebombed by seagulls. Note the imagery of a plane in the word "*jetting*" and the alliteration with "*jab*" for extra violence.

The poem ends with a bitter revelation. This visit to *Stewart Island* merely confirms a decision Adcock has already made – to leave New Zealand and return to England, the place of her childhood. In a sense, Adcock herself has been deceptive. Her description of Stewart Island, which appears to be spontaneous, if negative, is in fact a rationalisation of her decision, as if confirming to herself that it was the right one to make.

Presents from my Aunts in Pakistan – Moniza Alvi

Context

Moniza Alvi was born in Lahore, the capital of the Punjab region of Pakistan, in 1954, to an English mother and a Pakistani father. The family moved to England when she was a few months old. Here, Alvi was *"translated into an English girl"*, as she comments in her collection *"Souls"* (2002).

The poem also references the partition of India in 1947, along largely religious lines. Independence from Britain created the newly independent countries of India and Pakistan, which was divided into two non-contiguous regions - West and East Pakistan (later Bangladesh). There were recurring conflicts between India and Pakistan during the 1960s.

Themes

Alvi's poetry frequently explores issues of **identity and belonging.** In particular, she reflects on the **two cultures** of which she is a part. Links can be made with Nichols' *"Hurricane Hits England"*, and Adcock's *"Stewart Island"*, as both poets similarly emigrated to England in their youth. The poets evoke **a sense of the place in which they were born,** and **the importance of place in forming identity.** They compare or contrast the country of their birth with their adopted country .

Form, structure and language

This long poem is written in *free verse*. Alvi uses variations in line length to lead the reader through her poem and point up her images and ideas. It recalls her life as a teenager, reflecting on the gifts sent to her in England from Pakistan by her father's sisters. These gifts, and the objects her parents brought with them when they emigrated, prompt questions on the nature of identity and belonging.

The first stanza describes the gifts of clothes sent to Alvi; the second recalls her reaction to wearing them; in the third and fourth, she contemplates the objects brought by her parents from Pakistan and how they represent an alien culture; stanza five records the reaction of her friend to the clothes, which causes her to try and recapture her childhood; stanzas six and seven take on a darker tone as she imagines an alternative life as a woman in Pakistan.

In **the first stanza**, Alvi describes the clothes sent as a present by her aunts as attractive, exotic. The *"salwar kameez"* (long tunics with trousers) are made of colourful, shiny fabrics (*"peacock blue/glistening"*). The shoes are embroidered with gold and the bracelets are *"candy-striped"*. But these positive images are overlaid with negatives – the orange is *"split open"*; the shoes have *"points curling"* suggesting discomfort; the bracelets break and draw blood. The presents are both a gift and a threat to her peace of mind as she wrestles with her dual heritage.

Over time, the fashions in Pakistan change, as they do in England, and she can monitor the passage of time, as she grows up, through the gifts sent. However, both descriptions of the "*salwar bottoms*" are potentially negative – "*broad and stiff/then narrow*" suggesting confinement. When she becomes a teenager, the occasion is marked by the arrival of a "*sari*", a garment created by winding a long piece of fabric around the body, again restrictive. It is clearly expensive, bordered with "*silver*", but also "*apple-green*", and green apples are sour. Notice how Alvi places these images on separate, short lines, to point them up.

In **stanza two**, Alvi tries on the clothes and realises that they make her feel unlike herself ("*alien*") and somehow inferior, as if she can't quite measure up to their beauty. She wants the comfort of the familiar ("*denim and corduroy*"). The clothes she has been sent are a "*costume*", something put on as a disguise or as if she is in a play, emphasising their strangeness. With their bright colours they are like flames in which she is a phoenix, waiting to be reborn. But she cannot change as those clothes seem to demand – she is "*half-English*", and only half-Pakistani, unlike her "*Aunt Jamila*". She is trapped between two worlds.

In **stanza three**, Alvi expresses her fascination as a child with the objects brought by her parents from Pakistan when they emigrated. As with the clothes, images of beauty are overlaid with ugliness. The lamp made of camel skin is transformed into a thing of beauty when switched on, but she is aware of the cruelty that went into its making. Just as the camel has been sacrificed to create something new, albeit beautiful, so she feels her relatives desire to transform her into something other, regardless of the cost to her sense of self.

In **stanza four**, it is her mother's jewellery, brought from Pakistan as a wedding dowry, which contrasts Pakistan with England. Here, the precious, delicate gold bracelets become a target for thieves. The clothes are shut away in her cupboard, but she can feel them burning through the doors, as if demanding that she give in to her Pakistani heritage. By contrast, her aunts ask for cardigans from that iconic British store, *"Marks and Spencer"*. To them, jumpers are as exotic as the *salwar, sari* or *filigree*[26] are to Alvi.

In **stanza five**, Alvi tests the reaction of her friend to the clothes, who is unimpressed. She is more interested in the clothes Alvi wears when relaxing at the weekend – British clothes. Alvi, however, uses the real glass mirrors sewed into the clothes metaphorically, to get in touch with her Pakistani heritage, imagining herself as a Pakistani girl. She tries to glimpse her past – the child on the boat with her parents travelling to England. *"Prickly heat"* is an itchy inflammation of the skin caused by blocked sweat glands. Alvi arrives in England to live in the house of her mother's mother, uncharacteristically alone – another contrast with life in Pakistan.

Stanza six continues Alvi's quest to discover her Pakistani heritage and her identity. She looks at photos

---

[26] *Filigree* is gold which has been made into fine patterns like lace

of Pakistan and tries to place herself in them. In the 1960s, when she was a teenager, she reads about the conflicts between India and Pakistan that flared up periodically, their violence, and her visceral reaction to it, conveyed by the word *"throbbing"*. The images of Lahore where she was born are a mixture of fantasy and reality. She imagines her aunts in *purdah*, hidden away from the gaze of male strangers, wrapping the presents. There is a note of sadness in the image of the women, confined to *"shaded rooms"* with no hope of travelling the world, and the loving care with which they wrap the presents in *"tissue"* paper and send them across that world to their unseen niece.

The **last stanza** presents more negative images of the unequal role of women in her birthplace. There are *"beggars and sweeper-girls"* (girls who clean the streets) who live in poverty. Being of *"no fixed nationality"* she feels she cannot fully engage with either Pakistan or England, and imagines herself as condemned to view the world from the other side of a decorative, but screened, window (*"staring through fretwork"*),[27] outside both cultures, looking in.

Alvi is equivocal about her Pakistani heritage. On the one hand she is fascinated, but on the other she finds it frightening, as the alternating positive and negative images throughout the poem suggest. England is cosy and familiar, like the M&S cardigans coveted by her aunts; the gifts from Pakistan are fascinating and

[27] The *"Shalimar Gardens"* in Lahore were created in the 17th century and are now a World Heritage site.

seductive, but unsettling. As a teenager, Alvi struggles to find her own sense of self. This is made even harder by the tug-of-war between the two cultures.

Hurricane Hits England – Grace Nichols

Context

Grace Nichols was born in 1960 in British Guiana, now Guyana, part of the Guianas, a region on the north coast of South America. Nichols emigrated to England in the 1970s and is the partner of fellow Guyanese poet John Agard.

Guyana has strong ties with the culture and history of the Caribbean region. Many of the inhabitants are Afro-Guyanese, descendants of African slaves. The names of the Gods of the Winds invoked by Nichols derive from the Yoruba region of West Africa, from where many slaves were transported.

The *"Hurricane"* that hit England was in 1987, an event with a *return period* (likelihood of happening again) of 1 in 200 years. The winds, recorded up to 120 mph, devastated much of southern England. Millions of trees were downed and there were extensive power outages and property damage. Hurricanes are more usually weather systems found in the Caribbean region and Nichols imagines the winds bringing a message to the speaker from her homeland.

Themes

Many of Nichols's poems centre **on the importance of place in creating identity.** She uses the hurricane of 1987 as a way of linking her two cultures – Guyanese and British – and in so doing, she finds a way to reconcile herself to her exile from her homeland. The poem can be compared to Alvi's *"Presents..."* which also considers identity and dual heritage.

Form, structure and language

The poem is written in *free verse*. The first stanza is in the *third person*, as Nichols projects her own feelings about her Caribbean heritage onto a female *persona*. The remaining stanzas are in the *first person*, giving the woman's words as she prays to the spirits of the wind to give her their message, brought across the Atlantic.

In **stanza one**, the woman's estrangement from her adopted country, England, is revealed in the words *"It took..."*. Until the hurricane, she has felt like an alien in a strange land. It is this momentous event which allows her to finally connect with England – *"the landscape"*. She listens to the wind *"howling"*, the sound like the wind in the rigging of a huge, masted ship travelling across the oceans. The wind gains strength as it travels, approaching like a ghost from her ancestral past, both frightening and yet comforting, as it is familiar to her.

In **stanza two**, the *persona* calls out to the spirits, the *anaphora*[28]:of *"Talk to me "* like a prayer. *"Hurucane"* is a Native American word from which *hurricane* is derived, meaning an evil wind spirit; *"Oya"* is the spirit of the River Niger (in West Africa) and of the wind, lightning, fire and magic; *"Shango"* is the God of thunder and lightning; *"Hattie"* refers to Hurricane Hattie that struck Guyana in 1961, when Nichols was a

---

[28] Repetition at the beginning of successive clauses.

child, hence "*back-home cousin*". She pleads with the spirits to "*Talk*" to her; bring her some message from her homeland.

In **stanza three,** the woman rhetorically asks the wind spirits why they have come all the way to England – where they do not usually travel – to cause such destruction. What are they trying to tell her? They speak in their ancestral language ("*old tongues*") but are alien in England.

Stanza four continues the questioning – what is the meaning of the lightning flashes, that cause power-cuts, thus bringing both light and darkness together?

In **stanza five,** she questions the meaning of the uprooted trees. She continues the sea imagery of stanza one with the metaphor "*heavy as whales*" to describe the crash of them falling. Their roots are "*crusted*" with the earth dislodged as they fall, and they leave behind large holes ("*craters*") which are where they will die.

In **stanza six**, she expresses her feelings. Just as the Hurricane has disrupted normal weather patterns, so it has disrupted her emotions. She feels set free from old patterns of feeling – "*heart unchained*". She throws herself into the spirit of the storm, allowing it to take her where it will.

In **stanza seven,** she finds an answer. The "*mystery*" that the winds bring is "*sweet*" as it helps her understand herself better. She imagines herself to be like a landscape changed by the storm. The winds have stirred long-dead feelings within her ("*frozen lake*") and, like the uprooted trees, she has been shaken to her core. The message she reads in the wind is that the earth is a single place, even though we divide it into different continents and countries and thus artificially separate where we are born from where we now live. This realisation reconciles her to her former feelings of alienation in England by helping her to see that she is part of one world.

Nothing's Changed – Tatamkhulu Afrika

Context

There are few people who have had as many names as this poet or as eventful a life. Born Mohamed Fu'ad Nasif in 1920, in Egypt, to Turkish/Arab parents, he moved when a baby to South Africa and was adopted by white South Africans on the death of his parents. His adoptive parents called him John Charlton.

He fought in World War 2 and was captured and imprisoned at the siege of Tobruk in 1942. On his return to South Africa, he was adopted by Afrikaners and renamed Jozua Francois Joubert.

In 1964, he converted to Islam and took the name Ismail Joubert. He lived in District 6, a multi-racial, liberal, residential district in Cape Town[29]. In the 1970s, around 60,000 residents were forcibly removed, and the area razed to the ground by the apartheid regime. Apartheid was a system of racial segregation, based on white supremacy, that existed between the 1940s and 1990s. Measures against the integration of White, African, Indian and Coloured peoples (as designated by law) included the pass laws, a system of identification that controlled movement, bans on inter-racial marriage, segregated schools and transport as well as forceable removal to designated areas. Nearly all aspects of civil society were affected.

---

[29] "*District 9*" is a 2009 Sci-Fi movie based on District 6 and the forcible removal of its multi-racial occupants.

Joubert formed an anti-apartheid, armed resistance group – the *Al-Jihaad* - which later affiliated with the African National Congress (ANC). He was given the name "Tatamkulu Afrika" which is a 'praise name' meaning 'grandfather' or 'great father of Africa'.

He was imprisoned in 1987 for acts of terrorism and kept in the same prison as Nelson Mandela for eleven years until his release in 1992. He died in 2002.

Themes

The title *"Nothing's Changed"* is ironic. When the poem was written, legalised apartheid had been abolished, yet Afrika sees signs that racial segregation remains systemic in South African society. On the other hand, everything has changed since he was last in District 6, the once vibrant, multi-racial community reduced to a wasteland by the authorities to promote their policy of segregation. The poem explores **the importance of place in creating identity,** although Afrika's identity is perhaps more fluid than most. The poem also expresses how **a place can recall a particular time**, stimulating **memory**. It can be compared with Wordsworth's *"On Westminster Bridge"*, Thomas's *"Adlestrop"* or Hardy's *"Where the Picnic was"*, all of which **capture a particular moment in time in a particularised place.** Like Blake's *"London"*, the poem uses **place to convey a political message** about disadvantage and privilege.

Form, structure and language

Writing about his poetry , Afrika said: "*I am completely African. I am a citizen of Africa; I'm a son of Africa - that is my culture. I know I write poems that sound European, because I was brought up in school to do that, but, if you look at my poems carefully, you will find that all of them, I think, have an African flavour.*"

This poem is a masterpiece of sensuous imagery, particularly appealing to the auditory sense, and rich in English poetic techniques, particularly *alliteration* and *onomatopoeia.* It is comparable to the language of the poems of Keats, Wordsworth, Browning or Thomas. It also uses word-play to create rich, complex images.

The poem is in *free verse,* with the line length and line breaks carefully placed to contain an image or describe an emotion. It is in the *present tense*, which gives it a feeling of immediacy, as if we are walking with the poet. The six-stanza structure follows Afrika's walk across the wasteland surrounding the old District 6 to the beginnings of the new development that has sprung up in its place, signified by the new Hotel. Each stanza marks a stage in this walk and his response to what he sees and feels.

Stanza one evokes the sounds his footfalls make as he crosses the wasteland surrounding the old District 6. Note the *mono-syllabic* words of the opening line, dropped like pebbles, the use of *consonance*[30]: "*round*

---

[30] Repeated *consonants* – letters other than vowels

hard **st**ones" and the *onomatopoeic: "click"* to mimic the stones under his feet. In line 3, he moves off stony ground into long grass, using *sibilance* [31] to describe the sounds of the grasses brushing against his legs: "**seeding grasses thrust/bearded seeds**...". This sound imagery continues as he treads on discarded beer-cans, unseen in the long grass, with the repeated consonant "*c*": "**c**uffs, **c**ans/trodden on," and the final *onomatopoeic* "**crunch**". The final two lines shift attention to the tall grasses amongst which purple flowers bloom. Notice how the predominant *mono-syllables* give way to *polysyllabic* words, as he seems to lift his head from underfoot, with the "*small, hard stones*", to what lies around him, an expanse of grass and "*purple-flowering, /amiable weeds*". The weeds are "*amiable*" because, being of the natural world, they are politically and racially neutral and non-judgemental.

At the opening of **stanza two**, we are brought up short by the declamatory "*District 6*", as if it *were* a notice board. Afrika stops, realising where this walk has brought him – to the boundary of the old District 6. Although there is no sign, Afrika has a *visceral*[32] response to the place, feeling its presence in his body. Afrika uses *syndetic*[33] listing to emphasise the power of this physical response: "**and** my hands/**and** the skin.../

---

[31] Repeated "*s*" and "*sh*" sounds
[32] An involuntary physical response - like butterflies in the stomach, or a sick feeling.
[33] Using conjunctions to list, such as "*and*".

and *the soft.../**and** the hot..."*, each phrase lengthening as his anger grows.

In **stanza three**, he sees the new Hotel that has been built on the "*grass and weeds*" of his former community. Afrika uses *assonance*[34] on various "*a*" sounds to create an ugly, harsh sound, conveying the arrogance of those that built it and his anger at this symbol of continuing white supremacy: "*brash*", "*glass*", "*flaring*", "*flag*". It sits like a toad ("*squats*"), ugly and loathsome. The "*Port Jackson*" trees are imports, brought in to suggest class and money. They are "*incipient*"[35] because they are not yet fully grown; they may even be still wrapped in the sacking that protected them on their journey from the coast. Like the trees, the restaurant offers imported, French food ("*haute cuisine*") in its attempts to distance itself from the past, and the locals. There is even a "*guard at the gatepost*" to stop undesirable people entering – and that means people of colour. Afrika puns on the apartheid era signage that read "*Whites Only*" and "*inn (in)*" to show that although apartheid has legally ended, there are still overt symbols of racism within this new South African society. Just as he needed "*No board*" to tell him that he had entered District 6 (stanza two), he needs "*No sign*" to tell him that he, and people of his colour, are not welcome in this hotel. The phrase "*we know where we belong*" is a reference to the oft-chanted racist demand that POC "*go back where they*

---

[34] Repeated, rhyming vowel sounds
[35] *Incipient* means "*about to become*"

belong", which was also heard in the UK during the 1950s and 1960s, as well as in countries with institutionalised racism.

In **stanza four**, he approaches the hotel and looks through the windows, an outsider who can see "*clear*[ly]" what this place is telling him. He knows what he will see (note the emphasis on "*know*" placed at the end of the line) – further symbols of rich, White culture. Describing the table settings, the last three lines of this stanza are a masterpiece in manipulating language. Notice the absence of commas in the line "*crushed ice white glass*", which can be read in a number of ways, creating complementary images of *whiteness*: "*crushed ice/ice white/white glass*". Similarly, "*linen falls*" refers to the white linen tablecloth, but by using the word "*falls*" as both a noun and a verb, he conveys the idea of *waterfalls*, as it is long enough to spill (*fall*) over the table and cascade to the floor. This opulence contrasts with the simple phrase "*the single rose*", the understated, ubiquitous table decoration for "*up-market*" restaurants, suggesting both expense and yet refinement. This rose is not "*amiable*" like the weeds.

Stanza five contrasts these symbols of White culture with the lives of the POC who live just "*Down the road*" but a world apart. The lines take on a more accented, urgent rhythm as his anger at the ironic contrast between the two ways of living grows: "**Down** the **road/work**ing **man's cafe** sells/**bun**ny **chows**." A "*bunny chow*" is a stew which is held in a bowl made of bread, which is then eaten. "*Take it with you, eat*" is a subtle reference to the Holy Communion ("*Take...Eat*") suggesting that poor, working people are also God's children, but it is made ironic by the next line *"at a plastic table top"*. No linen tablecloth in this diner; people use their *"jeans"* (which were working clothes) to clean their fingers. The negative images of how poor, POC behave - or how they are believed to behave by White people - is rounded off with *"spit a little on the floor"*. *"It's in the bone"* again echoes the commonly held belief of the time that POC were genetically different from White people and, as a result, incapable of education and becoming successful businesspeople or leaders in their communities, and their country.

In **the final stanza**, Afrika feels himself reacting to the continuing, if less overt, apartheid of his youth with the same boiling anger he felt then. He backs away from the window, leaving a circle of his breath on the pane. He is aware that his anger diminishes him (*"small mean O/of small mean mouth"*), but he cannot help his visceral reaction, its intensity conveyed by *"burn"*. As a youth, he would have thrown a stone to shatter (*"shiver"*[36]) this glass wall between White and Black; as a man, and one who has committed terrorist acts, it would be a bomb. The final line references the title and is a bitter acknowledgement that although apartheid has been legally abolished, institutionalised racism is still prevalent in South African society.

---

[36] Plate glass does not break like the glass in a domestic window pane. It collapses from the top in a cascading motion – hence *"shiver"*.

Postcard from a Travel Snob – Sophie Hannah

Context

Sophie Hannah (born 1971) is a novelist, poet and academic perhaps best known for her internationally best-selling crime fiction, including a continuation of Agatha Christie's novels featuring the Belgian detective, Hercule Poirot. She has written several books of poetry and was short-listed for the TS Eliot Poetry Prize in 2007 with *"Pessimism for Beginners"* (Carcanet Press 2007). She has recently published a self-help book *"How to Hold a Grudge"* (Hodder & Staunton 2018). She is the daughter of children's author Adèle Geras.

Hannah was born in Manchester and lived in *"leafy, vibrant West Didsbury in the south of the city"*[37] until she was 19 and went to Manchester University. In the same interview with the Guardian, she reveals that she never believed she would ever leave Manchester: *"Why wouldn't I? Where else was there to go?"* It was not until she moved to Cambridge as a junior fellow that she realised *"how Manchester-only [her] formative years had been."* It is perhaps the insularity of her youth, and an appreciation of the life-changing effects of travel, that has prompted this ironic *dramatic*

---

[37] The Guardian Dec 2018
https://www.theguardian.com/books/2018/dec/01/made-in-west-didsbury-manchester-cambridge-live

monologue, which is a scathing commentary on the snobbery of a certain kind of British tourist.

The poem is taken from her 1997 collection *"Hotels like Houses"*.

Themes

The poem does not sit comfortably amongst others in this collection, as its primary theme is not *place* as such, but rather **social commentary**. The title tells us the poet's intention in writing the poem, which is to target those we might now call "eco-tourists" who scorn mass-market tourism whilst contributing to the environmental and social impact of global travel. As social commentary, it can be compared with Blake's *"London"*. Links can be made to Fanthorpe's *"First Flight"* which also shows contrasting attitudes to travel.

Form, structure and language

This *dramatic monologue* is predominantly in *iambic pentametre* with a regular *abab* rhyme scheme. The rhythm and rhyme both contribute to the tone of someone telling us "how it is" with an air of confident authority. However, Hannah uses *enjambment* to create the smug tone of the *persona* and to make ironic comments on her pretensions.

In **stanza one**, the poet subverts the usual opening greeting on postcards from travellers, as the *"travel snob"* asserts that she does NOT want others to be where she is – she wants exclusive access to her chosen destination. Not only that, she does not want to see it become a *"resort"*, a place created for mass tourism with entertainment designed for tourists. These '*resorts*' enable tourists to travel to other countries whilst enjoying familiar food and culture, isolating them from the local people and their customs. Her clichéd "*perish the thought*" suggests that, in spite of her pretensions, she is, in fact, rather an ordinary person.

Stanza two continues the idea of her wishing for solitude and exclusivity: "*peaceful*", "*untouched*". She uses hyphenated phrases to create *hyperbolic*[38] negative images of other places "spoiled" by mass tourism: "*seaside-town-consumer-hell*". Her commitment to an alternative travel experience is typified by where she stays, "*a local farmer's van*", which is a humorous exaggeration of where eco-tourists choose to stay, such as *yurts* or communal dormitories. Placing the comment "*it's great*" on the following line seems somewhat desperate, as if anticipating a negative response. The final phrase, exaggerating her isolation, is carried over to the next stanza, using *enjambment...*

In **stanza three,** another cliché ("*within a hundred miles*") suggests she is increasingly desperate to convince us (herself?) of the merits of her chosen travel experience. The '*Nobody speaks*" placed at the end of the line suggests loneliness rather than chosen solitude. Using *enjambment*, it is resolved with "*English*" on the following line, but she immediately justifies herself ("*rest assured*") with another hyphenated phrase,

---

[38] *Hyperbole* is a rhetorical term meaning exaggeration. The opposite is *litotes*, meaning understatement.

savagely characterising those tourists she sees as less "authentic" than her: *"sun-and sangria-two weeks-/small-minded-package-philistine-abroad)"*. Note the use of the alliterative *"sun and sangria"* as if she is spitting out her dislike.

The air of smug self-satisfaction returns in **stanza four**, with the assertion of her "multi-culturalism". The poet's use of irony is evident in how the *persona* chooses to illustrate this, which is through semantics – changing the words for things. If you are the kind of tourist the *persona* sees herself as being, and drink a lot of wine, you are a *"wine connoisseur"*, which is respectable, not simply a *"drunk"*, which is not. Similarly, and humourously, the despised tourists are just sea-bathers, whereas she is someone who studies the culture of other Peoples. She just chooses to be wearing swimming trunks to carry out her research.

In Romney Marsh – John Davidson

Context

John Davidson (1857-1909) was a Scots poet and former teacher who moved to London in his thirties and established himself as a writer of drama and poetry. He was particularly noted for his *"Ballads and Songs"* (1894) from which this *ballad* is taken. Whilst he had many admirers amongst his contemporaries, including the poet W.B. Yeats, underlying mental health problems and financial worries drove him to suicide by drowning.

The Romney Marshes are in the south-east corner of Kent and run into the sea at Dymchurch, from which they are separated by a seawall. At the time, Kent had extensive marshland which was drained for agriculture during the 19th and early 20th centuries. Further north was the landscape immortalised by Dickens in *"Great Expectations"* (1860-1): *"The marshes were just a long black horizontal line then, as I stopped to look after him; and the river was just another horizontal line, not nearly so broad nor yet so black; and the sky was just a row of long angry red lines and dense black lines intermixed."* Davidson captures the same landscape of endless skies and changing light in this *ballad*.

In his later works, Davidson used many references to science, in which he had been interested from an early age. This can be seen in his reference to the *"wire"* – the telephone lines which would have been a new addition to the landscape as this technology developed at the turn of the century.

Themes

Although the poem is a *ballad*, which is usually a narrative poem, telling a story, this poem reads more as a *lyric* poem, **evoking landscape**. The narrative element is in the progression from going *"down to Dymchurch Wall"* and *"came up from Dymchurch Wall"*, suggesting a passage of time in which the light on the marshland changes from daylight to sunset. The lyrical description can be compared to Wordsworth's *"On Westminster Bridge"* or Thomas's *"Adlestrop"*, but it perhaps lacks their emotional intensity. Davidson is clearly fascinated by the unique qualities of the light and sound of the Marsh, but, arguably, as detached observer. There is little sense of the transcendent – an experience which takes the poet out of himself into a new understanding of self in relation to his surroundings. The *ballad* form, with its regular rhythm and rhyme, perhaps contributes to this distancing.

Davidson also suggests by his description of the sound of the wire in the wind that **new technology can be integrated into an ancient landscape**, becoming part of it, as much as the *"masts"* of ships, an older technology. Similarly, it is the *"express-train"*, another relatively new technology at the turn of the 20th century, that brings Thomas into contact with the landscape around him in *"Adlestrop"*, as he listens to the *"steam hiss"*. Wordsworth, too, is able to express delight in the potential beauty of the scientific, man-made world with its *"Ships, towers, domes, temples"*. These ideas can be contrasted with Fanthorpe's in *"First Flight"* where the aircraft takes her outside *"Familiar England"*, to an alien landscape of clouds and air where *"nothing lives"*. Similarly, Blake suggests that London's inhabitants are alienated from the natural world by the corrupting influence of commerce and industrialisation, expressed in *"the charter'd Thames"* and *"mind-forged manacles"* that destroy natural feelings of compassion and fellow-feeling. Lastly, Afrika contrasts the *"amiable weeds"* growing in the old District 6 with the *"incipient Port Jackson trees"*. The *"weeds"* grow naturally in the abandoned District whilst the *"trees"* are an alien import by Whites, symbolising the ugly social and political divisions within this society.

Form, structure and language

Ballads are traditionally narrative poems written in *common metre* – stanzas of four alternating lines of *iambic tetrametre* and *iambic trimetre*, as in Dickinson's *"I Started Early..."*. However, this poem is written in a variant called *long metre*, four lines of *iambic tetrametre*, with a rhyme scheme *abab*. *"Adlestrop"* also uses long metre. The opening is typical of ballads – the *persona* tells of a walk or journey undertaken which leads to a happening that becomes the subject of the poem. The riddling rhyme *"As I Travelled to St Ives"*, or WH Auden's *"As I Walked Out One Evening..."* and Dickinson's *"I Started Early..."* all open with this device.

Davidson makes extensive use of colour and sound imagery to evoke the unique landscape of the Marsh.

In **stanza one**, the poet walks across the Marsh towards the sea and the *"Dymchurch Wall"* which separates it from the English Channel. He hears the South wind blowing over the Marsh and sees the sunlight (in the west) glowing on the walls of the churches which rise above the flat, open marshes as they are on small hills (*"knolls"*). *"Norman churches"*, such as St Mary in the Marsh, are those built by the Normans after the invasion of William the Conqueror in 1066, which led to the Battle of Hastings, a town a few miles south-west of Romney Marsh. The reference to *"yellow"* sunlight is the first of many uses of colour in the poem.

In **stanza two**, he hears the sound of the wind whistling in the telephone wires which are strung across the marsh, between the towns of Romney and Hythe, the sound conveyed by the *assonance* of *"ringing shrilly"*.

In **stanza three**, he paints a colour picture of the bands of light along the horizon as sunset approaches – the *"purple "* ribbons of cloud, above which there is a brighter *"sapphire"* (bright blue) band and above that a pinkish, *"rose"* light that fills the sky (*"Heaven's gates"*). This is strongly reminiscent of Dickens' description of the *"lines"* of red and black he sees in the sky above the marshes.

Stanza four looks out towards the sea where the poet can see the masts of ships moving to-and-fro in the wind (*"wagged"*) and hear the sound of the waves breaking on the shore – likened to the regular rhythm and sound of a peal of bells (*"swinging/pealed"*). The sound is echoed as the sea retreats back down the beach (*"prolonged the roar"*). The colour imagery continues with the adjective *"saffron"*, a deep yellow, and is enriched by images of gems – *"diamond/beads"*, linking back to *"sapphire"* – suggesting the sparkling spray.

In **stanza five**, the poet begins his return journey away from the beach, with the sun now setting in the west across the Weald of Kent and the South *"Downs"*. The colour imagery continues with *"crimson"*, the setting sun likened to the dying of a red fire (*"brands/flicker"*), the metaphor intensified by the *alliterated "fall /Flicker /fade"*.

The sudden onset of darkness is conveyed by the *disyllabic* opening to **stanza six**: *"Night sank;"*. The imagery of fire is continued with the *simile "like flakes of fire"* to describe the brilliance of the stars against the night sky. Again, he hears the *"shrill"* sound of the wind in the wire.

The **final stanza** returns to sounds of the sea on the beach behind him, now *"darkly shining"*[39]. Davidson this time uses the *onomatopoeic "clashed"* to describe the sound of waves breaking on the shore, whilst the answering sound of the beach as the sea withdraws is now likened to the sound of a church organ with the *"stops"* pulled full out, to give maximum volume.

---

[39] An *oxymoron,* where two contradictory words are juxtaposed.

Absence – Elizabeth Jennings

Context

Elizabeth Jennings (1926-2001) was an English poet who spent most of her life in Oxford and was a devout Roman Catholic. She was considered part of *"the Movement"*[40], a group of post-war English poets that included her friends Philip Larkin and Thom Gunn, who favoured simple, unadorned language whilst using traditional metric forms. The poem is taken from the collection *"A Sense of the World"* published in 1958, following travel in Italy made possible by winning the Somerset Maugham Prize for poetry a few years earlier.

Whilst Jennings claimed that her poetry was not autobiographical, saying: *"Art is not self-expression while, for me, 'confessional poetry' is almost a contradiction in terms."*[41], many of Jennings' poems are about love and relationships, her parents and death, which are clearly drawn from her own experiences.

Themes

Like others in the collection, the poem shows the close **relationship between place and memory** and how places enable us to recall emotions first experienced

---

[40] So-called as the result of being included in an anthology of poetry *"New Lines"* (1956) compiled by the critic Robert Conquest.
[41] As quoted in the *Daily Telegraph* obituary (2001) and at http://elizabethjennings.dmu.ac.uk which contains an extensive study of her life and work.

there. Similarly, powerful emotions are recalled by Afrika in "*Nothing's Changed*" when he returns to the place where he grew up, and Hardy's "*Where the Picnic Was*" where he recalls a lost love and happier times. It is a reflection on **Time Past, Change, and Loss**.

The poem also explores how **emotions can affect perceptions of both time and place**. Jennings reflects on how the external landscape – here, a garden – can seem physically unchanged ("*Nothing was changed*"), and yet her relationship to it is utterly different, as a result of a traumatic experience. Links can be made to Hardy's "*Where the Picnic Was*", where the familiar setting is overlaid with feelings of loss and sorrow and it appears "*cold*" and "*grey*", even though it is recognisably "*the same*". In contrast, Afrika claims that "*Nothing's changed*", referring to the political landscape, whereas the physical landscape is unrecognisable, as a formerly vibrant community has given way to "*stones*", "*grasses*" and "*weeds*". Adcock's perceptions of "*Stewart Island*" are tainted by her negative attitude towards New Zealand, finding ugliness beneath a picture-postcard-perfect landscape.

Form, structure and language

Like her fellow Movement poets, Jennings wrote in simple language using traditional metric forms with regular rhyme. The poem is written in three *quintets*. The underlying rhythm of the poem is *iambic pentametre.* The rhyme scheme is a regular *ababa,* using full rhymes, which gives each stanza a sense of being complete in itself. In addition, many of the lines seem to fall into two, complementary halves, as below:

"I visited the place   where we last met
Nothing was changed   the gardens were well-tended

This adds to the tight rhythmic structure, which, together with the rhyme scheme, gives the poem a tone of emotions kept tightly under control, a deadening of emotion until the contrast of the revelation of the depth of her feelings through the words *"savage force/earthquake tremor/shaken"* in the final stanza.

Stanza one opens with a simple statement of the circumstances that have given rise to the poem – revisiting the place of a final meeting with someone close to the speaker. The formal gardens with their *"fountains"* are as they were when they last met; outwardly *"nothing was changed"*. All is as usual and there are no signs that she should feel differently. Notice how natural the rhythms of her speech seem, in spite of the rigid metric and rhyming structure. This is created partly by the use of *caesura* in line 2 after *"changed"*, giving the two-part structure to the line noted above, and by the mixture of *end-stopping*[42] and the use of *enjambment* across lines 4 and 5.

In **stanza 2**, the speaker's emotions begin to affect her perception of the garden. The birds are *"thoughtless"* because they continue to sing in spite of her loss. She

---

[42] Ending the sense of a line at the end of a line – so, a sentence corresponds to a line, as in line 1

cannot share in their joy but is puzzled as to why not ("*Played cunning on my thoughts*"). Surely this garden is so beautiful and peaceful ("*Pleasures/level*") that it can disperse sad and unwelcome thoughts?

In **stanza three**, the speaker explains her feelings. It is precisely because the garden seems so unaffected by the "*absence*" of her lover/friend that she feels it so deeply – "*a savage force*". The calm appearance of the garden is shattered by her loss: "*an earthquake tremor*". All the elements of the garden that made it pleasurable, "*fountain, birds and grass/…shaken*" to the core.

Links, Connections, Comparisons & Tackling the Unseen Poem

The exam question (the "task")

The exam question will give you a "*theme*" to discuss as a guide to which aspects of the poem(s) they want you to focus on. They may ask you to focus on a particular *poetic technique*. They will probably use the word "*Compare*". Where possible, links and connections should be made to each poem throughout the essay, alternating between the two, for the highest marks. The examiners are less keen on one analysis followed by another, unless there is clear cross-referencing and/or there is a clearly comparative paragraph at the beginning and at the end.

What is happening in the poem?

The first task is to understand "*What is happening in the poem?*" Unless you understand this, your analysis will be meaningless. Make sure you understand what the story, incident, event or imaginative idea is that has prompted the poet to write the poem. No poem exists in a vacuum – there is always a reason for writing it. Find that reason – the inspiration which leads to the poem.

The first "link or connection" to be made is to summarise, briefly, the "story" of each poem *and how this relates to the theme of the question*. This is the first response to "*How*" the poet has approached his subject. It is the framework around which he hangs his ideas. It is suggested that you do this in your first paragraph. It also reassures the Examiner that your analysis is not starting from an erroneous base. **Make the "story" the first point of comparison between the texts.**

What is the relevant context within which the whole poem is written?

Make any immediate comparisons of "**context**". Are the poems addressing the same themes but within **a different time-frame** (past/present, for example)? Is there any relevance of the theme to our **experience today which is different to theirs**? Are the poets writing in a literary **tradition**? What do you know about **the poets' lives** that is relevant and may be a cause for writing the poems? Are there any **specific events** that the poems are referring to?

Ensure that you always relate context back to the question. They do not want, for example, a history of Romantic poetry – but they do want you to show that you understand their **predominant concerns and styles** and **how this is reflected** in the poetry.

As you discuss **form, structure and language**, refer to any relevant **contextual factors that affect the choice of these elements**. For example, the use of classical or religious imagery reflecting a literary tradition or societal norms; use of language forms, such as *dialect*, that are used to convey the message of the poem.

Form, structure and language

A poem may have many ideas in it. Your task is to explain **how the poet has used form, structure and language to explore the theme which is the focus of the question**. Below are some of the features of the poems that you can choose to explore, both when making links, connections and comparisons between the prescribed poem and one other from the *Anthology*, AND when linking the two Unseen poems.

Remember that the highest marks are given when the analysis of form, structure and language is related to meaning and to the theme under discussion. Fewer marks are given for merely identifying techniques in isolation from meaning. The commentaries on the poems show you how to do this.

It is important that you use *"examples"* (quotes) to illustrate your argument. Never make a comment about how the poet has approached his subject without an example to illustrate. You should also ***never use a quote without then going on to talk about the quote*** itself, analysing any structural or language features in depth and ***relating this to the writer's intention***. This ensures that you are covering the assessment objective AO2 – *"showing a critical understanding of the writer's craft."* However, comments like *"paint a picture in your mind"* or *"make the reader feel sorry for..."* are too general to gain credit at the higher levels. You need to be specific about why a writer has chosen a language or structural feature.

Theme	The question will focus on a theme (or occasionally a poetic technique). Some key themes have been identified in the commentary on the texts. Choose poems which can be linked thematically as a first choice for linking, connecting and comparing. Trying to link poems "because you know them" is not a good plan.
Context	Is there a historical /biographical /literary /political/ social-economic background that is relevant to the text and the way it is written? **How does the context of the text relate to the meaning of the text and help us to understand it?**
Narrative Voice	Who is speaking in the poem? Is it the poet, or is he speaking through someone else? Is there more than one *voice*? The narrative voice is the person who is speaking in the poem. It may be the poet (many of the poems are autobiographical) or a *persona* – an imagined speaker, as in a *dramatic monologue*. Or it may be the poet simply talking to us about an idea that he/she wishes to explore. **What does the choice of narrative voice tell us about the poet's approach to his theme or about the theme itself?**

Form	Is the poem written in a named poetic form, such as *sonnet, ode, elegy, ballad*? **What does the choice of form tell you about the subject matter or the attitude of the poet?**
Structure	How many lines are there in a stanza? How is the story arranged around these lines?
	What is the subject matter of each stanza? In what order has the story or happening been told to us? Are there shifts in time or place?
	Is there a regular rhythm? If so, what is this rhythm?
	Is there a regular rhyme scheme?
	Are *full rhymes, half-rhymes* and *eye-rhymes* used?
	Are the lines *end-stopped* – does the meaning follow the rhyme and complete at the end of each rhymed line?
	Does the poet use *enjambment* and *caesura* to vary the pace of the line and create a looser structure within a rigid one? What does this say about the subject matter or the poet's attitude to his subject?
	Is it in free verse, with no discernible regular rhyme or rhythm?
	How has the poet chosen where to end the lines?
	How does the choice and use of structure relate to meaning and what is the effect on the reader?

Language	Is the language formal or informal? Does it sound conversational, confiding, reminiscent, musing, purposeful…?
	What is the tone? Sorrowful, regretful, angry, puzzled, triumphant…?
	What is the proportion of *vernacular* (words of common speech) to Latinate (polysyllabic, Latin derivations, "difficult")?
	Is the language descriptive, factual, plain, colloquial …?
	Is the language literal, or does it have many *similes* and *metaphors*, or *personification*?
	What kinds of *imagery* are used? Religious, naturalistic, mechanistic…?
	Are there particular words used which are unusual? Archaic, *dialect*, slang …?
	How does the choice and use of language relate to meaning and what is the effect on the reader?

A Note on Metre

Rhythm in English Verse

Rhythm in English verse is dependent on the **pattern** and **number** of *stressed* and *unstressed* syllables in a line. This is called *metre*. The name given to the *metric line* depends on **a)** the pattern of *stressed* and *unstressed* beats in the *metric feet* and b) the number of *metric feet* in a line. If the pattern changes in a line, the predominant pattern is used to define it.

Pattern

Each pattern of *stressed* and *unstressed* syllables has its own name. In the examples, the *stressed* syllables (or *beats*, as in music) are highlighted. The symbol "/" divides the line into its *metric feet*.

"I **wan**/dered **through**/ each **char**/ter'd **street**
Near **where**/ the **char**/ter'd **Thames**/ does **flow**"

Here, there are four *metric feet* in each line, each with the pattern "light/**HEAVY**" or "ti-**TUM**". This makes it a *metric line* of four *iambs* – *iambic tetrametre*.

Iamb – unstressed, stressed (ti-**TUM**). *"I star/ted Ear/ly – Took /my Dog..."* which is a regular *iambic* line. It is the most common *foot* found in English poetry. Dickinson's line above is *iambic tetrametre* – four feet of *iambs*.

Trochee – stressed, unstressed (**TUM**-ti). **"Marks of/weak**ness**/, marks** of **/woe"** which is in *trochaic tetrametre* - four feet of *trochees*[43].

Spondee – stressed, stressed (**TUM-TUM**). *"Night sank"*. The use of the *spondee* gives weight to the words, matching the meaning.

Dactyl – stressed, unstressed, unstressed (**TUM**-ti-ti). An example of a *dactyl* is in the word *"Liverpool"*

Anapaest – unstressed, unstressed, stressed (ti-ti-**TUM**) *"The As**syr**ian des**cend**ed like the **wolf** on the **fold**"*, which is a regular *anapaestic* rhyme.

Amphibrach – unstressed, stressed, unstressed (ti-**TUM**-ti) as in Cope's *"1st Date"*: *"I **said** I /liked **classi**/cal mu*sic/. This is an unusual metric form.

Counting *metric feet*

In Dickinson's lines above, there are four *metric feet*. The number of *metric feet* is given a name derived from Greek metrics, as below:

The numbers of *feet* in a line are called:

Trimetre – 3	Hexametre - 6
Tetrametre - 4	Heptametre - 7
Pentametre – 5	Octametre – 8

---

[43] See also *"catalectic"* which is an abbreviated form of this line

A *catalectic* line is one where the last, or first, part of a metric foot is missing. This is most clearly seen in Blake's "*London*":

And **mark**/ in **ev**/ery **face**/ I **meet**
Marks of /**weak**ness,/**marks** of /**woe**.

The first line has four clear *iambic* feet – ti-**TUM** – which makes it *iambic tetrametre.* However, the second line has three clear *trochaic* feet (**TUM**-ti) – plus an extra stressed syllable at the end (**woe**). This unfinished metric foot is called *catalectic*. If it were finished, it would make a line of *trochaic tetrametre.* However, looked at another way, you could say that it is the FIRST syllable of an *iambic tetrametre* line that is missing, hence "*headless*":

Marks/ of **weak**/ness, **marks**/ of **woe**/

Note that the last syllable of the *headless* or *catalectic* line has a long vowel or a *dipthong*: *woe (line 4), walls (line 12), tear (line 15).* This also serves to disguise the shortening of the metric line.

Metric Forms or Names (given in order of prevalence)

Iambic pentametre – is the commonest metric form in English and comprises a *metric line* of *five iambic feet.* Variation is given by the use of other *feet*, which can give the verse the sound of natural speech rhythms. However, the *five-foot, iambic pattern* is always underlying.

NOTE: you will hear people describe *iambic pentametre* as containing ten unstressed/stressed *syllables*. This is not the case. **It has nothing to do with the number of syllables** – only the number and type of the *feet*. This example (from Wordsworth's *"Extract..."*) makes this clear:

"The hori/zon's **bound**,/ a **huge**/ peak, **black**/ and **huge**,/"

There are **eleven** syllables – the extra syllable given by the *anapaest* (ti-ti-**TUM**) *"The hori/zons..."* – in an otherwise *iambic pentametre* line.

Blank verse is *unrhymed iambic pentametre,* commonly used by Shakespeare, but also by Seamus Heaney and other modern poets who write in a classic tradition.

Iambic tetrametre is four *iambic* beats in a line, as used by Thomas in *"Adlestrop":*

"Yes, **I** /re**mem**/ber **Ad**/le**strop**"

Tetrametre is also the rhythm of many nursery rhymes. We describe this as "sing-song" as it is common in songs and light verse. The four-beat **iambic tetrametre** line may alternate with a three-beat **iambic trimetre** as in **common** or **ballad metre,** used by Dickinson in "I started Early – Took my Dog":

"I **star**/ted **Ear**/ly – **Took**/ my **Dog** – "
And **vi**/**sited**/ the **Sea!**"

This *metre* can be used ***ironically*** by poets when dealing with a serious subject, so watch out for a deliberate mismatch between the metre and the subject matter to make a point.

End-stopping is where the sense of the line, contained in a clause or sentence, ends at the end of the line, where the *metric line* ends, as in Jennings's *"Absence"*:

"I visited the place where last we met.
Nothing was hanged; the gardens were well-tended
The fountains sprayed their usual steady jet;"

This tends to emphasise rhyme, making it more insistent, as here to convey the heaviness of the scene.

Enjambment is the opposite of *end-stopped*. The sense of the line continues onto the next line, often landing on a stressed beat, to emphasise the first word of the line, and enhance meaning, as here in Jenkins's poem:

"   Surely in these
Pleasures there could not be a pain to bear"

Here, the enjambment causes the reader to land on the *"Pleasures"*, emphasising the *oxymoron* of *"Pleasures/pain."*
Enjambment also tends to propel the verse forwards, making it flow, even if there is a regular rhyme scheme.

Free verse is a modern form of poetry that has no **regular** *rhythm* or *rhyme*. However, if there were neither rhythm nor rhyme, then one might as well call it prose, divided up into arbitrary lines. *Free verse* frequently uses *enjambment* and *caesura* to guide the reader through the argument and create rhythmic and rhyming effects, as here in *"First Flight..."*:

"A sudden swiftness, earth slithers
Off at an angle."

Printed in Great Britain
by Amazon

66542313R00068